Newcastle
City Council

Newcastle Libraries and Information Service

 **0845 002 0336**

Due for return	Due for return	Due for return
˙- 8 SEP 2011		
29/11		

Please return this item to any of Newcastle's Libraries by the last
date shown above. If not requested by another customer the loan
can be renewed, you can do this by phone, post or in person.
Charges may be made for late returns.

easy hot & spicy

favourite fiery dishes from around the world

RYLAND
PETERS
& SMALL

LONDON NEW YORK

First published in the United Kingdom in 2008
by Ryland Peters & Small
20–21 Jockey's Fields
London WC1R 4BW
www.rylandpeters.com

10 9 8 7 6 5 4 3 2

ISBN: 978-1-84597-631-6

Printed and bound in China

A CIP catalogue record for this book is available from
the British Library.

Senior Designer Paul Tilby
Senior Editors Julia Charles, Clare Double
Picture Research Emily Westlake
Production Paul Harding, Patricia Harrington
Art Director Leslie Harrington
Publishing Director Alison Starling

NOTES:

All spoon measurements are level unless otherwise specified.

Ovens should be preheated to the specified temperature.
If using a convection oven, cooking times should be
reduced according to the manufacturer's instructions.

Uncooked or partly cooked eggs should not be served to the
very young, the very old or frail, or to pregnant women.

Speciality Asian ingredients are available in larger
supermarkets and Asian stores.

To sterilize preserving jars, wash them in hot, soapy water
and rinse in boiling water. Place in a large saucepan and
then cover with hot water. With the saucepan lid on,
bring the water to a boil and continue boiling for
15 minutes. Turn off the heat, then leave the jars in the
hot water until just before they are to be filled. Sterilize
the lids for 5 minutes, by boiling, or according to the
manufacturer's instructions. Jars should be filled and
sealed while they are still hot.

contents

feel the burn...

Whether you fancy a curry with a kick or an exotically spiced tagine, you're sure to find something perfect here. These quick and easy recipes have been specially chosen to help even the busiest people enjoy delicious, fresh, home-cooked food.

Hot and spicy dishes are so much more than one element, and they vary in flavour as much as they do in colour. An incredible variety of chilli peppers and herbs and spices is used to create the tastebud-tingling flavours that you find in fiery food from around the globe. India, Thailand, China, North Africa, Mexico, South America and Spain are just some of the countries and regions represented here, and all of them have a tradition of tasty, spicy food – the very best of which you'll find in this recipe collection.

Included are great ideas for deliciously different party nibbles and food for sharing plus simple recipes for starters and light lunches. For the health conscious, fish and seafood dishes make a good choice, as they are light on calories but big on taste. Meat eaters will enjoy the more substantial dishes, from delicious beef curries to a slow-cooked tagine – perfect for a cosy night in. Chicken dishes are great for everyday eating throughout the year, from a warming Thai curry to something spicy cooked on the barbecue in summer. Food for vegetarians is also brought to life with the addition of heat – try one of the spicy Mexican bean dishes or a crisp Chinese stir-fry.

So why not turn up the heat in your kitchen and discover how exciting sizzling hot and aromatic food from around the world can be.

small bites and dips

500 g uncooked prawns, shelled and deveined

4 kaffir lime leaves, very finely chopped

4 spring onions, finely chopped

2 tablespoons chopped coriander

1 egg

1 tablespoon Thai fish sauce

50 g rice flour

peanut or sunflower oil, for frying

chilli jam

500 g ripe tomatoes, coarsely chopped

3–4 red chillies, coarsely chopped

2 garlic cloves, chopped

1 teaspoon grated fresh ginger

2 tablespoons light soy sauce

250 g palm sugar or soft brown sugar

100 ml white wine vinegar

½ teaspoon sea salt

2 preserving jars, about 200 ml each, sterilized

serves 6 (makes 24)

Thai fish, prawn or crab cakes are quick and easy to make – perfect as a first course or as a spicy snack with drinks. If you have time, marinate the prawn mixture for 30 minutes or so. To make this recipe simpler, you can use a prepared chilli sauce.

thai prawn cakes
with chilli jam

To make the chilli jam, put the tomatoes, chillies and garlic into a food processor and purée until fairly smooth. Transfer to a saucepan, add the ginger, soy sauce, sugar, vinegar and sea salt and bring to the boil. Cook for 30–35 minutes, stirring occasionally until thick and glossy.

Warm the jars in a low oven, pour in the thickened jam and let cool completely. Seal and store in the refrigerator.

To make the prawn cakes, put the prawns into a food processor and blend to a purée. Add the lime leaves, spring onions, coriander, egg, fish sauce and rice flour, blend briefly and transfer to a bowl. Using damp hands, shape the mixture into 24 patties, 5 cm diameter.

Pour 1 cm depth of the oil into a frying pan, heat for 1 minute over medium heat, then add the cakes, spaced apart. Fry in batches for 2 minutes on each side until golden brown. Remove, drain on kitchen paper and keep them warm in a low oven while you cook the remainder. Serve with chilli jam or sweet chilli sauce.

Prawns make the fastest, most impressive dish you can imagine. If you want to use precooked prawns, just sprinkle them with the chilli oil and lemon juice and serve with the cool and refreshing pesto.

prawns with chilli oil
and pistachio and mint pesto

To make the pesto, put the nuts, mint, garlic and spring onions into a food processor and grind coarsely. Add the oil and purée until fairly smooth and green. Stir in the vinegar and season to taste. Set aside while you prepare the prawns, or store in the refrigerator for up to 5 days.

Put the prawns into a shallow dish and sprinkle with the chilli oil and salt and pepper. Cover and let marinate for at least 30 minutes or longer, if possible.

When ready to serve, thread the prawns onto skewers and cook on a preheated barbecue or stove-top grill pan, or under a hot grill, for about 2 minutes on each side until charred and tender – the flesh should be just opaque. Do not overcook or the prawns will be tough.

Arrange on separate plates or a large platter, sprinkle with the lemon juice and serve with the pesto and crusty bread to mop up the juices.

24 large uncooked prawns, shelled and deveined

4 tablespoons chilli oil

freshly squeezed juice of 1 lemon

crusty bread, to serve

pistachio and mint pesto

50 g shelled pistachio nuts

a bunch of fresh mint

1 garlic clove, crushed

2 spring onions, chopped

125 ml extra virgin olive oil

1 tablespoon white wine vinegar

sea salt and freshly ground black pepper

4 skewers

serves 4

2 spicy chorizo sausages

20 freshly shucked oysters

shallot vinegar

3 tablespoons red wine vinegar

2 tablespoons finely chopped shallot

1 tablespoon snipped chives

sea salt and freshly ground black pepper

cocktail sticks

a large platter filled with ice cubes

serves 4

This combination may sound slightly unusual, but it is totally delicious. Fresh oyster, a nibble of hot sausage and a sip of chilled dry white wine is a taste sensation – try it, you'll be amazed.

oysters with spicy chorizo

To make the shallot vinegar, put the ingredients into a bowl and mix well. Pour into a small dish and set aside until required.

Preheat the grill, then cook the sausages for 8–10 minutes or until cooked through. Cut the sausages into bite-sized pieces and spike them onto cocktail sticks. Arrange in a small dish. Put the oysters into their half-shells and arrange on the ice. Serve with the chorizo and shallot vinegar.

These little fried cakes of potato and chorizo with a crisp corn salsa are based on a Mexican dish using queso fresco, a mild fresh cheese. This recipe substitutes fresh goats' cheese, which has an affinity with spicy food though it isn't traditional. You could also use feta cheese, as long as it's not too salty.

tortitas de papa
with chorizo
and corn salsa verde

Put the potatoes in a large saucepan, bring to the boil, then simmer for 15–20 minutes or until tender. Drain well and when cool enough to handle, peel and pass through a potato ricer, mouli or a sieve into a large bowl.

Heat a non-stick frying pan, add the chorizo and sauté gently for 5–10 minutes until the fat renders. Lift out the chorizo with a slotted spoon, let it cool slightly, then add to the bowl of potato. Add the garlic, spring onions and goats' cheese and mix. Add the egg and salt and pepper and mix well.

Divide the mixture into 18 parts and form into small flat cakes. Roll each potato cake in the breadcrumbs, pressing gently so the crumbs stick. Set aside while you make the salsa.

To make the salsa verde, put the mustard in a small bowl and whisk in the lime juice. Continue whisking, adding the olive oil in a thin stream until amalgamated. Stir in the remaining ingredients, then add salt and pepper to taste.

Heat the oil in a large frying pan and fry the potato cakes in batches until golden brown all over (about 8–10 minutes). Drain on kitchen paper and keep warm while you cook the remaining potato cakes.

Serve with the salsa and a crisp salad.

750 g potatoes, unpeeled, scrubbed well

3 chorizo sausages, peeled and crumbled

1 garlic clove, crushed

4 spring onions, chopped

250 g goats' cheese, crumbled

1 egg, beaten

75 g fine dry breadcrumbs

olive oil, for frying

sea salt and freshly ground black pepper

corn salsa verde

1 tablespoon Dijon mustard

1 tablespoon freshly squeezed lime juice or wine vinegar

150 ml extra virgin olive oil

2 tablespoons capers, rinsed and chopped

75 g canned sweetcorn kernels, drained

2 spring onions, finely chopped

1–2 garlic cloves, very finely chopped

6 tablespoons chopped flat leaf parsley

6 tablespoons chopped coriander

1–2 green chillies, finely chopped

sea salt and freshly ground black pepper

serves 6 (makes 18)

750 g large floury potatoes, peeled

2 green chillies

½ teaspoon dried red chilli flakes

1 small onion, finely chopped

1 teaspoon salt

1 teaspoon ground cumin

1 teaspoon ground turmeric

2 tablespoons chopped coriander

25 g unsalted butter, melted

150 g plain flour

vegetable oil, for frying

coconut and mint chutney

125 g grated fresh coconut or
75 g unsweetened desiccated coconut

200 g plain yoghurt

1 green chilli, deseeded and chopped

2 tablespoons chopped mint

½ teaspoon salt

½ teaspoon sugar

serves 8–10 (makes 64)

India has dozens of different kinds of bread – plain, flavoured with spices as here, or with spicy fillings. They are served with curry or dhal, but these roti are made smaller to eat as a snack. You could continue the potato theme and serve roti with vodka-based drinks – vodka is sometimes made from potatoes, as well as from grains.

mini potato roti
with coconut and mint chutney

If using desiccated coconut to make the chutney, put it in a bowl and cover with warm water. Let soak for about 20 minutes, then strain through a sieve, pressing the coconut against the sieve to squeeze out any excess moisture.

Put all the chutney ingredients in a bowl, mix well and set aside.

Cook the potatoes in boiling salted water, drain and mash well. Deseed and finely chop the fresh chillies. Add to the potatoes and stir in all the remaining ingredients, except the flour, and mix well. Gradually mix in the flour until you have a soft dough. Divide the dough into 64 small, equally sized pieces. Taking one piece at a time roll out on a floured board to a 7 cm circle. Continue with the remaining pieces of dough.

Heat a little oil in a heavy-based frying pan and cook the roti 2 or 3 at a time for 1–2 minutes on each side until lightly browned all over. Keep warm in a low oven while you cook the remainder. Serve with the coconut and mint chutney.

¼ teaspoon pasilla chilli flakes,
with seeds

1 chipotle chilli, deseeded and chopped

6 thick slices jalapeño in brine
or 1 large fresh jalapeño, deseeded

150 g cabbage (about 5 large leaves),
trimmed of tough stalks

1 small onion

1 tablespoon chopped oregano
or marjoram

3 tablespoons white wine vinegar

3 tablespoons rice vinegar

5 tablespoons pineapple juice

sea salt, to taste

serves 6 as a relish

This crunchy relish from Mexico is made with three chilli varieties, revealing their individual flavours – liquorice-like pasilla chilli flakes, smoky chipotle chillies and jalapeño slices – but you could use just the jalapeño and one other.

chilito

Soak the dried pasilla and chipotle chillies in 2 teaspoons warm water for about 15 minutes, then drain. Finely chop the jalapeños. Set aside.

Finely shred the cabbage in a food processor and transfer to a bowl. Repeat with the onion and add to the bowl. Add the oregano, chillies and salt and toss well.

Mix the vinegars and juice in a small jug and add to the bowl. Mix very well (the liquid is just enough to coat the vegetables – it is not meant to submerge them). Set aside for 1–2 hours to develop the flavours. Serve a little chilito on the side with Mexican main course dishes, burritos or corn chips, and other condiments.

This sauce or condiment is always on hand in Mexico. Add it to anything you think needs a bit of livening up, or serve with corn chips and margaritas or Bloody Marys.

salsa roja

Break the chillies in half and shake out the seeds. Heat the oil in a frying pan, add the chillies and fry until they turn bright red. Remove with a slotted spoon and put into a bowl. Cover with water and let soak for about 30 minutes.

Add the garlic to the pan and fry until golden. Transfer to a food processor, add the drained chillies and chop coarsely. Add the oregano and tomatoes and chop again. Add salt and pepper to taste and serve with corn chips.

12 dried New Mexico chillies (or other mild dried chillies)

125 ml sunflower oil

3 garlic cloves, halved

1 tablespoon chopped oregano

6 large, ripe tomatoes, skinned and deseeded

sea salt and freshly ground black pepper

corn chips, to serve

makes about 500 ml

Vietnam is known for its delicate cuisine. It is notable for its great use of herbs, while spices, when used, are balanced and often gentle. Typical in southern cooking are spices such as ginger, galangal, star anise, tamarind, chillies and occasionally turmeric, five-spice powder and curry powder. This appetizing starter of stuffed baby squid, spiced with star anise, ginger and pepper, is a fine example. Nuóc cham is the traditional Vietnamese dipping sauce, but you could also use soy sauce or chilli sauce.

vietnamese spiced squid

To make the dipping sauce, use a mortar and pestle to grind the garlic, chilli and sugar to form a paste. Stir in the lime juice, fish sauce and about 3 tablespoons water. Transfer to a dipping bowl.

To prepare the stuffing, pour boiling water over the noodles and let soak for 4 minutes or according to the instructions on the packet. Drain well, coarsely chop the noodles and transfer to a large bowl.

Put 1 tablespoon of the peanut oil into a wok, heat well, swirl to coat, then add the spring onions, ginger and garlic. Stir-fry for a few minutes until softened, then add to the noodle bowl. Chop the squid tentacles and add to the ingredients in the bowl. Add the pork, star anise, fish sauce, sugar, salt and ¼ teaspoon of cracked black pepper and mix well.

Stuff the squid bodies, leaving a little space at the top. Secure closed with cocktail sticks.

Heat the remaining oil in a frying pan and add the squid. Cook gently for 10–12 minutes, until lightly browned in places and cooked through.

Slice the squid or leave them whole. Serve with fresh herbs and the nuóc cham.

Note To prepare the squid, cut off the tentacles and reserve. Cut off and discard the eye sections. Rinse out the bodies, discarding the tiny transparent quill. If you can't find squid with tentacles, buy an extra body, chop it coarsely, then add to the stuffing mixture.

25 g cellophane rice noodles (rice vermicelli), about 1 small bundle

90 ml peanut oil

3 spring onions, chopped

3 cm fresh ginger, peeled and grated

2 garlic cloves, chopped

16 prepared, cleaned baby squid with tentacles reserved*

325 g pork mince

2–3 'petals' of 1 star anise, finely crushed (about ¼ teaspoon ground)

1 tablespoon Thai fish sauce

a pinch of sugar

sea salt and cracked black pepper

a handful of mixed Asian herbs, to serve

nuóc cham dipping sauce

1 garlic clove, crushed

1 red bird's eye chilli, thinly sliced

2 tablespoons sugar

freshly squeezed juice of ½ lime

4 tablespoons Thai fish sauce

cocktail sticks

serves 4–6 (makes 16)

250 ml Chinese glutinous rice*
by volume, or about 200 g

1 teaspoon salt

1 teaspoon sugar

2 teaspoons white rice vinegar

60 g firm tofu

1 garlic clove, crushed

3 cm fresh ginger, peeled and grated

2 tablespoons light soy sauce

2 tablespoons sweet chilli sauce

2 tablespoons peanut oil

6 eggs, beaten

6 asparagus spears or 12 green beans,
cooked, about 75 g

3 spring onions, halved lengthways

soy sauce mixed with a little grated
fresh ginger, to serve

serves 4–6 (makes 24)

*Glutinous rice is sold in Asian food
stores. If unavailable, Japanese sushi
rice can be used – or even pudding rice.*

Egg fried rice is a popular Chinese dish and Japanese sushi makes excellent party food. This recipe mixes the two together. Make these rolls in the morning and keep them chilled until 30 minutes before serving.

egg rolls with chilli tofu

Pour 500 ml water into a medium saucepan, bring to the boil, then add the rice and salt. Reduce the heat to a low simmer, cover and cook for 12 minutes without lifting the lid. Remove from the heat and let stand for 5 minutes. Put the sugar and vinegar in a small bowl or cup, stir to dissolve, then mix into the rice. Let cool.

Cut the tofu into 5 mm slices. Arrange in a single layer in a flat dish. Put the garlic, ginger, soy and sweet chilli sauce in a small jug, mix well, then pour over the tofu. Set aside to marinate for 10 minutes.

Heat 1 tablespoon of the oil in a large frying pan, add the tofu and cook for 1½ minutes on each side. Remove from the pan, cut the slices into 5 mm strips, then set aside.

Heat 1 teaspoon of the remaining oil in the same frying pan and add one-third of the beaten egg. Swirl the egg around to cover the base of the pan and cook for 2 minutes until set. Carefully remove the omelette to a plate and cook the remaining egg mixture in the same way in 2 more batches.

Stretch a piece of clingfilm (about 10 cm longer than your omelette) on a flat surface and put 1 omelette in the middle. Spread with one-third of the rice. Close to the near edge, arrange a line of tofu, asparagus and spring onions – use one-third of the ingredients for each omelette. Carefully roll up the omelette, pulling away the clingfilm as you go. Wrap in the clingfilm until ready to serve.

Unwrap the rolls and slice into 2–3 cm pieces. Serve with the soy sauce.

You can use either fresh squid or frozen, whole or cleaned, for this – though if they're cleaned, they won't have their pretty flowerlike tentacles. Squid is equally good, if not better, after being frozen – freezing serves the same purpose as the fisherman beating the fish against a stone to tenderize it.

spicy crumbed squid strips

If using fresh squid, you will need to clean it first. Pull the tentacles out of the body, then cut off the rosette of tentacles – you may need to press out the tiny hard piece from the middle of the rosette. Keep the tentacles and bodies and discard the rest. Pull the pen (the transparent 'spine') out of the body and discard it. You can remove the thin purplish skin if you like, but it is edible. Rinse the bodies, pat dry and cut lengthways into 4–6 strips.

Put the breadcrumbs, garlic, ginger, parsley, chillies, five-spice and salt in a bowl and mix well. Mix the eggs and soy sauce in a second bowl.

Fill a wok or saucepan one-third full with the oil and heat to 180°C (350°F), or until a small cube of bread turns golden in 45 seconds. Dust the squid with flour, dip into the egg, then the breadcrumb mixture. Fry in batches of 8 for 2–3 minutes, then remove and drain on crumpled kitchen paper. Keep them warm while you cook the remainder.

Serve with sweet chilli sauce.

6–8 medium (15–20 cm) squid, about 400 g

75 g fresh breadcrumbs

2 garlic cloves, crushed

3 cm fresh ginger, peeled and grated

a small bunch of parsley, finely chopped, about 15 g

2 red or green chillies, finely chopped

2 teaspoons five-spice powder

1 teaspoon salt

2 eggs, beaten

2 tablespoons soy sauce

peanut oil, for frying

flour, for dusting

sweet chilli sauce, to serve

serves 4–6 (makes 32)

Chilli beef makes a great filling for wontons, which are more traditionally filled with minced pork and prawns. They can be fried in advance and reheated in the oven at 190°C (375°F) Gas 5 for 8 minutes before serving.

crispy chilli beef wontons

To make the filling, slice the steak into thin strips and, if they are wider than 1 cm, slice them in half lengthways. Put in a bowl and mix in the sesame oil, vinegar and oyster sauce.

Using a small food processor or mortar and pestle, grind the chillies, ginger, garlic and salt to a coarse paste. Add to the steak, mix well and set aside for about 30 minutes.

Put 1 tablespoon of filling in the centre of each wonton wrapper, brush around the edges with the egg white and gather up, twisting to seal.

Fill a wok or frying pan one-third full with the oil and heat to 190°C (375°F) or until a small cube of bread turns golden brown in 30 seconds. Cook the wontons in batches of 6 for 2–3 minutes until golden and crisp. Drain on crumpled kitchen paper, then serve with plum sauce.

500 g sirloin or blade steak

1 tablespoon sesame oil

2 teaspoons white rice vinegar

3 tablespoons oyster sauce

2–4 red chillies, deseeded and chopped

4 cm fresh ginger, peeled and chopped

3 garlic cloves

1 teaspoon salt

32 large wonton wrappers*

1 egg white, beaten

peanut oil, for frying

plum sauce, to serve

serves 4–6 (makes 32)

Packets vary, but contain about 40 large (10 cm) or 70 small (8 cm) wrappers. Leftovers can be frozen.

500 g minced pork

6 garlic cloves, crushed

2 stalks lemongrass, thinly sliced

1 bunch coriander, finely chopped

2 red chillies, deseeded and chopped

1 tablespoon brown sugar

1 tablespoon Thai fish sauce

1 egg, beaten

salt and freshly ground black pepper

peanut oil, for frying

chilli dipping sauce

125 ml white rice vinegar

2–6 small chillies or 1 large red chilli, thinly sliced

1 tablespoon Thai fish sauce

1 spring onion, thinly sliced (optional)

½–1 tablespoon brown sugar

serves 4

A delicious main course served with other Asian dishes, and also great at a drinks party. Use fat Fresno chillies for a mild flavour, or bird's eye chillies for blinding heat.

thai pork balls
with chilli dipping sauce

Mix all the ingredients for the chilli dipping sauce in a small bowl, stir to dissolve the sugar, then set aside to develop the flavours.

To make the pork balls, put all the remaining ingredients, except the peanut oil, in a bowl and mix well. Dip your hands in water, take about 1–2 tablespoons of the mixture and roll it into a ball. Repeat with the remaining mixture.

Fill a wok one-third full of peanut oil and heat until a cube of bread browns in 30 seconds. Add the pork balls, 6 at a time, and deep-fry in batches until golden brown. Remove and drain on crumpled kitchen paper, keeping them warm in the oven until all the balls are done. Serve with the chilli dipping sauce.

For this dish only the thick part of the chicken wings is used, marinated in a blend of lemongrass and chilli. The crunchiness of the deep-fried lemongrass makes an interesting texture. The winglets are simple to prepare. Run a knife around the narrow end of the wing, just below the knuckle, then use your knife to cut and push the flesh down the bone to form a little ball at the bottom. The bone then acts as a handle, perfect for finger food.

chicken wings
with lemongrass and sweet and hot sauce

3 stalks of lemongrass, finely chopped

2 small chillies, finely chopped

3 tablespoons oyster sauce

1 tablespoon Thai fish sauce

1 teaspoon sugar

500 g chicken winglets
(also known as drumettes)*

peanut or sunflower oil, for deep-frying

sprigs of coriander, to serve

sweet and hot sauce

4 tablespoons sugar

6 tablespoons rice vinegar

½ teaspoon salt

2 small red chillies, finely chopped

an electric deep-fryer (optional)

serves 4

Put the lemongrass, chillies, oyster sauce, fish sauce and sugar in a bowl and beat with a fork. Add the chicken winglets, turn to coat and set aside to marinate for 15 minutes.

Meanwhile, make the sauce. Put the sugar, vinegar and salt in a saucepan and heat, stirring, until the sugar dissolves. Add the chillies and 4 tablespoons water, stir well and simmer until it becomes a thin syrup. Pour into a dipping bowl.

Fill a wok or deep-fryer one-third full with the oil or to the manufacturer's recommended level. Heat until a scrap of noodle will puff up immediately.

Working in batches if necessary, fry the chicken winglets until golden brown. Remove with a slotted spoon, drain and serve with the sweet and hot sauce and sprigs of coriander.

*Note If you are unable to find chicken winglets, buy the whole wings and cut off the last 2 joints. Use them for another recipe or to make stock.

Thai dips are mostly made from chillies. They are used both as dipping sauces and for spooning over rice or other dishes. This dip, as its name implies, is made from young, green, strongly flavoured chillies and is wonderful to serve with drinks at parties. Deseed the chillies if you like.

vegetables
with spicy Thai dip of young chillies

Wrap the chillies, garlic, shallots and tomatoes in foil and put under a preheated medium grill. Cook until they begin to soften, turning once or twice. Unwrap, then pound with a mortar and pestle to form a liquid paste.

Add the lime juice, soy sauce, salt and sugar to the paste, stirring well, then spoon into a small dipping bowl.

Serve as a dipping sauce surrounded by crisp salad ingredients, such as lettuce, cucumber, radish and celery, or with raw or blanched vegetables.

4 large green chillies

4 small green chillies

6 large garlic cloves

6 pink Thai shallots or 3 regular ones

4 medium tomatoes

2 tablespoons freshly squeezed lime or lemon juice

2 tablespoons light soy sauce

½ teaspoon salt

2 teaspoons sugar

your choice of salad or other vegetables, to serve

serves 4

2 green chillies

1 large red or green pepper

250 g feta cheese, thickly sliced

4 tablespoons extra virgin olive oil

freshly squeezed juice
of 1 small lemon

3–4 tablespoons milk

1 teaspoon hot red chilli flakes

1 tablespoon finely chopped
flat leaf parsley

freshly ground black pepper

toast or crudités, to serve

a metal skewer

serves 6

The name of this Greek dish, tyrohtipiti, means 'beaten cheese'. It originated in the beautiful city of Thessaloniki, but is fast becoming popular all over Greece. Its colour varies according to the type of peppers used and the heat of the chillies. It can be pink or red; in Thessaloniki it is green, as is the version here.

feta and chilli dip

Thread the chillies on a metal skewer and put over a low gas flame or on a preheated barbecue. Turn them over until scorched. Put the pepper over the flame and do the same until it feels soft and partially scorched. The pepper will take longer than the chillies. Set aside until cool enough to handle.

Deseed and peel the red pepper and do the same with the chillies, which will be a little more difficult. Wipe off any blackened bits with kitchen paper. (Beware of the hot chillies.)

Put the chillies, pepper, feta, olive oil, lemon juice, milk and black pepper in a food processor and blend until creamy. If the mixture is too stiff, add a little more milk. Remove to a plate or bowl, sprinkle the chilli flakes and parsley on top and chill lightly. Serve with toast or crudités.

This spicy Middle Eastern chickpea dip is good served simply with grilled pita bread or with spicy kebabs or garlicky grilled poussin. It is always present among the exotic array of dishes on meze tables everywhere from Beirut to Byblos.

spicy hoummus

Drain and rinse the soaked chickpeas and put them in a saucepan. Cover with plenty of water, bring to the boil and skim until clear. Cover and cook until perfectly soft, about 1 hour.

Strain the chickpeas, reserving 300 ml of the cooking liquid. If using canned chickpeas, strain them first and discard the liquid, but use about 4 tablespoons cold water in the food processor.

If the tahini paste appears separated in the jar, mix it well first. Divide all the ingredients into 2 batches and put the first batch in a food processor, then process briefly. Ideally it should still have some texture and should not be too solid. Taste and adjust the seasoning with salt and pepper and blend again briefly. Transfer to a bowl and repeat with the remaining ingredients.

Trickle a little oil over the top and sprinkle with fresh coriander. Serve at room temperature with pita bread or triangles of toasted bread. In the summer, it is better served lightly chilled.

175 g dried chickpeas, soaked in cold water overnight, or 800 g canned chickpeas

2 tablespoons tahini paste

2 garlic cloves, chopped

freshly squeezed juice of 1–2 lemons

1 tablespoon ground cumin

2 tablespoons extra virgin olive oil

sea salt and freshly ground black pepper

to serve

1 tablespoon extra virgin olive oil

1 tablespoon coriander, finely chopped

pita bread or toast

serves 6

4 sprigs of coriander

4 sprigs of mint

75 g gram flour

pinch of turmeric

pinch of sugar

1 egg white

freshly squeezed juice of 1 lime

pinch of sea salt

250 g cauliflower

175 g courgettes

1 bunch of baby carrots

vegetable oil, for deep-frying

coriander chilli mint raita

4 sprigs of mint

4 sprigs of coriander

2 green chillies

1 cm piece of fresh ginger

1 garlic clove, crushed

2 limes

pinch of sea salt

4 tablespoons yoghurt

an electric deep-fryer (optional)

serves 4

Wonderful as party food, these light fritters also make perfect starters. Vary the vegetables to suit yourself, and serve with this wonderful raita with a hint of chilli.

vegetable fritters
with coriander
chilli mint raita

To make the raita, roughly chop the mint and coriander and put in a mixing bowl. Deseed and chop the chillies, peel and grate the ginger and add to the bowl with the garlic. Add the grated zest and juice of the limes, together with the salt and yoghurt. Mix and chill until ready to serve.

To make the batter, first chop the coriander and mint, then put in a bowl with the flour, turmeric and sugar. Whisk the egg white until stiff, carefully fold in the spiced flour, stir in the lime juice, salt and enough water to give a light batter.

Break the cauliflower into florets, cut the courgettes into 2.5 cm slices and trim the carrots. Heat the oil in a deep-fryer or saucepan.

Dip each piece of vegetable into the batter and deep-fry in hot oil until golden brown. Drain on kitchen paper. Serve hot with the raita.

Spring rolls are best served immediately after cooking, but to keep last-minute preparation minimal, make the filling up to 24 hours ahead. Fill the spring roll wrappers about an hour before cooking; keep them covered so they remain moist until cooked.

mini spring rolls
with chilli dipping sauce

2 tablespoons sunflower oil

50 g carrots, cut into matchsticks

50 g mangetouts, cut into matchsticks

50 g shiitake mushrooms, chopped

2.5 cm fresh ginger, peeled and grated

1 small red chilli, deseeded
and chopped

50 g beansprouts

2 spring onions, thinly sliced

1 tablespoon light soy sauce

2 teaspoons plain flour

8 x 20 cm square spring roll wrappers

oil for deep-frying

chilli dipping sauce

5 tablespoons sweet chilli sauce

1 tablespoon light soy sauce

an electric deep-fryer

serves 4 (makes 16)

Heat the sunflower oil in a wok or frying pan and stir-fry the carrots, mangetouts, mushrooms and ginger for 1 minute. Add the chilli, beansprouts and spring onions and stir-fry for 1–2 minutes, or until the vegetables are tender-crisp. Remove from the heat, stir in the soy sauce and set aside to cool.

Next, make the chilli dipping sauce. Mix together the sweet chilli sauce and soy sauce and transfer to a serving dish.

In a small bowl, mix the flour with 1 tablespoon water to make a paste. Cut the spring roll wrappers in half diagonally and place under a damp cloth to keep moist. Remove one at a time to fill.

Divide the filling into four and put a quarter of one batch on the long cut side of a wrapper, placing it along the centre, slightly in from the edge. Fold over the side flaps. Brush a little flour paste on the pointed end of the wrapper. Roll up towards the point, pressing the end to seal. Repeat with the remaining wrappers. Keep covered until ready to cook.

Fill a deep-fryer with oil to the manufacturer's recommended level. Heat the oil to 180°C (350°F) and deep-fry the rolls in batches for 2–3 minutes, until crisp and golden. Drain on kitchen paper. Serve hot with the chilli dipping sauce.

Aromatic skewers of meat, fish, vegetables and poultry are ubiquitous street food all over South-east Asia – and popular starters in restaurants too. Satays are easy to make – great for a party and delicious as part of a barbecue.

singapore pork satays

Using a sharp knife, cut the pork into 2 cm slices, then cut each slice into 2 cm cubes and set aside.

Put the coriander seeds in a dry frying pan and heat until aromatic. Using a mortar and pestle, grind to a powder. Alternatively, use a spice grinder or clean coffee grinder. Transfer to a wide bowl, then add the turmeric, salt and sugar.

Put the lemongrass and shallots into a spice grinder or blender and process until smooth (add a little water, if necessary). Add to the bowl and stir well. Stir in 2 tablespoons of the sunflower oil.

Add the cubes of meat and toss to coat with the mixture. Cover and set aside to marinate in the refrigerator for 2 hours or overnight.

Thread 2 pieces of pork onto each soaked wooden skewer and brush with the remaining sunflower oil. Cook under a preheated hot grill or over medium-hot coals on a barbecue. Thread a piece of cucumber onto the end of each skewer and serve with dipping sauce.

1 kg boneless pork loin

1 tablespoon coriander seeds

½ teaspoon ground turmeric

1 teaspoon salt

1 tablespoon brown sugar

1 stalk of lemongrass, trimmed and thinly sliced

5 small shallots, finely chopped

125 ml sunflower or peanut oil

1 cucumber, quartered lengthways, deseeded, then sliced crossways

dipping sauce such as soy sauce or nuóc cham (page 22), to serve

20 bamboo skewers, soaked in water for at least 30 minutes

makes 20

500 g beef steak

125 ml coconut milk

grated zest and freshly squeezed juice of 2 limes

2 red chillies, finely chopped

3 stalks of lemongrass, trimmed and finely chopped

3 garlic cloves, crushed

1 teaspoon ground cumin

2 teaspoons ground coriander

1 teaspoon ground cardamom

2 tablespoons Thai fish sauce or soy sauce

1 teaspoon sugar

sunflower or peanut oil, for brushing

dipping sauce, such as soy sauce or nuóc cham (page 22), to serve

10 bamboo skewers, soaked in water for at least 30 minutes

makes about 10

These beef skewers are also delicious made with other meats such as chicken, duck or pork. You could also serve them with the well-known satay sauce, made with peanuts, which is especially common in Indonesia.

indonesian beef satays

Using a sharp knife, cut the beef crossways into thin strips, about 0.5 cm thick and 5 cm long. Put the coconut milk, lime zest and juice, chillies, lemongrass, garlic, cumin, coriander and cardamom into a bowl, then stir in the fish sauce and sugar. Add the beef strips and toss to coat. Cover and chill in the refrigerator for 2 hours or overnight to develop the flavours.

Drain the beef, discarding the marinade. Thread the beef in a zigzag pattern onto the soaked skewers and cook under a preheated hot grill or in a frying pan (brushed with a film of oil) until browned and tender. Serve on a platter with a small bowl of dipping sauce.

soups and salads

This is a wonderful meal-in-a-bowl that takes only minutes to put together. It is quite spicy, so reduce the quantity of chilli if you prefer. Tom yum paste is a treasure to have in your storecupboard if you have a fondness for Thai food. Use it in stir-fries or Thai curries.

tom yum prawn noodle soup

100 g uncooked large or king prawns, shells on

2 tablespoons tom yum paste

1 red chilli, deseeded and finely chopped

1 red pepper, deseeded and thinly sliced

100 g brown cap mushrooms, sliced

100 g leeks, trimmed and finely diced

100 g rice noodles

freshly squeezed juice of 1 lime

a few coriander sprigs, to garnish

serves 2–4

Peel the prawns and use a very sharp knife to cut each one along the back so that it opens out like a butterfly (leaving each prawn joined along the base and at the tail). Remove the black vein.

Bring 570 ml water to the boil in a large pan. Stir in the tom yum paste until dissolved. Add the chilli, red pepper, mushrooms and leeks and let the mixture simmer for 5 minutes.

Meanwhile, put the noodles in a large heatproof bowl, cover with boiling water and leave to sit for 3–5 minutes until just tender. Drain and spoon into deep serving bowls.

Add the prawns to the tom yum mixture and simmer for a further 2–3 minutes. Pour the tum yum soup over the noodles. Squeeze a little lime juice over each bowl and garnish with a coriander sprig. Serve immediately.

4 ears of corn or 475 g fresh or frozen kernels

25 g butter

1 onion, finely chopped

1 small celery stick, finely chopped

4–5 slices back bacon, chopped

1.25 litres vegetable stock

250 ml single cream

cajun spice blend

¼ teaspoon each of black and white peppercorns

½ teaspoon each of cumin seeds, coriander seeds, cayenne pepper, paprika and celery salt

to serve

2 tablespoons chopped oregano

an extra pinch of Cajun spice blend

serves 4

Chowders are creamy, chunky soups, the most famous of which is New England clam chowder. Corn chowders are popular too – a real taste of America. This one is inspired by the Deep South: the result is Louisiana soul food with just the right amount of Acadian (Cajun country) spice.

cajun-spiced chowder
with corn and bacon

First make the spice blend by crushing the whole spices with a mortar and pestle until coarsely ground. Add the remaining ingredients and mix well.

If using fresh corn, remove the husks and silks and cut the stalk end flat. Put the flat end on a board and cut off the kernels from top to bottom. Discard the cobs.

Melt the butter in a large saucepan, add the onion and sauté for 5 minutes. Add the celery and sauté for a further 3 minutes until well softened. Add the bacon and cook for 1–2 minutes. Add the corn and 1½ teaspoons of the Cajun spice blend and mix well.

Add the vegetable stock and bring to the boil. Reduce the heat and simmer for about 35 minutes. Add the cream and simmer until thickened. You can serve the soup immediately or, to thicken it further, put a ladle of the chowder (without any of the bacon) in a blender and purée until smooth. Pour the blended chowder back into the saucepan and mix well.

To serve, ladle into bowls and top with a little oregano and a very light dusting of Cajun spice blend. Serve hot with crusty bread and a green salad.

2 tablespoons extra virgin olive oil

1 onion, chopped

3 thin celery sticks, chopped, with leaves reserved

1 large carrot, chopped

2 garlic cloves, chopped

250 g chorizo, skinned, halved, then cut into 1 cm slices

400 g canned chickpeas, drained

1.75 litres chicken stock

¼ teaspoon hot pimentón (Spanish oak-smoked paprika)

125 g spinach, tough stalks removed and leaves coarsely chopped

¼ teaspoon saffron threads, bruised with a mortar and pestle

Manchego or Parmesan cheese, shaved, to serve (optional)

serves 4

This hearty soup is a meal in itself. Chunks of chorizo float alongside chickpeas and spinach in a slightly smoky, fragrant broth. The special flavour comes from two typically Spanish spices, pimentón (Spanish oak-smoked paprika, made from a variety of capsicum or pepper) and its home-grown luxury spice, saffron. Although saffron is grown in many parts of the world, it is said that the best comes from La Mancha in Central Spain.

andalusian chickpea soup
with chorizo, paprika and saffron

Heat the oil in a large saucepan and add the onion, celery and carrot. Gently sauté the vegetables until they begin to soften. Add the garlic, chorizo, chickpeas, stock and pimentón. Bring to the boil, reduce the heat and simmer for about 10 minutes. Add the spinach and celery leaves and simmer for a further 15 minutes.

Add the saffron and clean out the mortar using a little of the stock. (It is a shame to waste even the tiniest speck of expensive saffron!) Add to the saucepan and simmer for another 5 minutes. Serve hot in large, wide bowls as a main course lunch. Add shavings of cheese, if using. This soup is very filling, but some good crusty bread and perhaps some extra cheese make delightful partners.

singapore turmeric laksa

To make the laksa paste, put all the ingredients in a blender or mortar and pestle and grind to a thick, chunky paste. If using a blender, add a little water to let the blades run.

Heat the oil in a large saucepan and add the laksa paste. Sauté for about 8 minutes. Add the chicken stock, lemongrass, lime leaves and lemon balm, if using, ginger and soy sauce. Bring to the boil and add the coconut milk, stirring to keep it from separating. Reduce the heat and simmer gently for 15 minutes.

Cook the noodles according to the instructions on the packet and drain.

Add the prawns, beansprouts, sugar and salt to the saucepan. Simmer for 2–3 minutes, until the prawns are just cooked. Discard the lemon balm and lemongrass and add the chopped coriander.

Deseed the cucumber and slice into matchsticks. To serve, put the noodles, cucumber and Chinese leaves into 4 large or 6 smaller bowls, then ladle over the soup.

Laksa, the spicy prawn and noodle soup from Malaysia and Singapore, has become fashionable all over the world. This one is a speciality of the Nonya or Straits-Chinese community. Its bright yellow colour comes from turmeric and, on its home ground, fresh turmeric is often used rather than the ground turmeric found in the West.

2 tablespoons peanut oil

1.5 litres chicken stock

1 stalk lemongrass, halved lengthways

2 kaffir lime leaves (optional)

2 long sprigs of lemon balm (optional)

4 thin slices of fresh ginger or galangal

1 teaspoon light soy sauce

400 ml canned coconut milk

250 g thick Chinese egg noodles

500 g uncooked prawns, shelled and deveined

125 g beansprouts

brown sugar or palm sugar, to taste

sea salt

a bunch of fresh coriander, chopped

laksa paste

6 shallots, coarsely chopped

4 red chillies, deseeded and chopped

1 stalk lemongrass, trimmed and chopped

1 teaspoon ground turmeric

1 garlic clove, chopped

½ teaspoon ground ginger or galangal

½ teaspoon anchovy paste

6 macadamia nuts or 12 almonds

1 kaffir lime leaf (optional)

2 tablespoons Thai fish sauce

to serve

10 cm cucumber

a handful of Chinese leaves, shredded

serves 4–6

750 g trimmed braising beef,
cut into small chunks

7 white peppercorns

3 cm fresh galangal, peeled and sliced,
or fresh ginger

1 teaspoon freshly grated nutmeg

¼ teaspoon ground turmeric

325 ml canned coconut milk

sea salt

spice paste

2–3 tablespoons peanut oil

1 teaspoon ground coriander

7 white peppercorns

4 red bird's eye chillies

2 teaspoons brown sugar

1 garlic clove, chopped

5 fresh Thai basil (or sweet basil) leaves

a large handful of fresh coriander,
about 25 g, coarsely chopped

8 pink Thai shallots or 1 regular shallot

a few cardamom seeds (not pods)

2 cm fresh ginger, peeled and chopped

1 teaspoon anchovy paste

1 tablespoon fish sauce

serves 4–6

This strongly spiced and flavoured soup has slices of meat swimming in plenty of creamy broth. It is quintessentially Indonesian in its spicing; living on the world's largest archipelago and comprising around 350 ethnic groups, Indonesians are a varied people and so is their cuisine.

indonesian beef and coconut soup

Put all the spice paste ingredients in a blender or a food processor and grind to a thick paste, adding a dash of water to keep the blades turning if necessary.

Put the beef, peppercorns, galangal, nutmeg, turmeric and salt into a saucepan, add 1.5 litres water and bring to the boil, skimming off the foam as it rises to the surface. Stir, reduce the heat and simmer uncovered for about 1½ hours, until the meat is mostly tender and the stock is well reduced.

Strain the beef, discarding the galangal slices and peppercorns, but reserving the stock. Return the stock to the pan, then stir in the spice paste. Bring to the boil, reduce the heat, add the beef and simmer for 5 minutes, stirring regularly.

Finally, add the coconut milk and simmer gently for a few minutes. Serve the soup on its own or with a small mound of plain rice.

2 garlic cloves

1 teaspoon coarse sea salt

30 cm cucumber, coarsely chopped

1 yellow pepper, deseeded and coarsely chopped

2 celery sticks, coarsely chopped

4 ripe tomatoes, coarsely chopped

1 red onion, coarsely chopped

1 litre fresh tomato juice

2 teaspoons cumin seeds, pan-toasted

1 teaspoon mild chilli powder

1 ripe avocado, halved and pitted

freshly squeezed juice of 2 limes

freshly ground black pepper

coriander leaves set in ice cubes or chopped coriander, to serve

serves 6

Ice-cold and enhanced with avocado, lime, cumin and chilli, this gazpacho is refreshingly hard to beat on a hot summer's day. If you have time, freeze coriander leaves in ice cubes and use them to decorate your soup.

mexican gazpacho

Using a mortar and pestle, pound the garlic with the salt until puréed. Put the cucumber, pepper, celery, tomato and onion in a bowl, add the puréed garlic and mix well. Transfer half of the mixture to a food processor and pulse until chopped but still slightly chunky. Pour into a large bowl. Purée the remaining mixture until smooth, then add to the bowl. Mix in the tomato juice, cumin, chilli powder and freshly ground black pepper to taste.

Chill for several hours or overnight, until very cold. If short of time, put the soup in the freezer for 30 minutes to chill.

Cut the avocado into small cubes, toss in the lime juice until well coated, then stir into the gazpacho.

To serve, ladle the soup into chilled bowls, then add a few ice cubes or sprinkle with chopped coriander.

This makes a lovely change from prawn cocktail! Buy the juiciest-looking cooked prawns you can find and leave them in the marinade for as long as possible. If it is available, use pink grapefruit; it looks prettier and tastes sweeter than the white variety.

chilli tiger prawn salad

1 garlic clove, crushed

freshly squeezed juice of 1 lime

2 tablespoons sweet chilli sauce

200 g cooked tiger prawns, peeled but tails left intact

1 pink grapefruit

2 tablespoons extra virgin olive oil

100 g cherry tomatoes, halved

1 small, ripe avocado, peeled, stoned and diced

½ red onion, thinly sliced

a handful of coriander leaves

serves 2

First prepare the prawns. Put the garlic, lime juice and sweet chilli sauce in a shallow, non-metallic container and whisk with a fork to combine. Add the prawns, stir to coat with the mixture, cover and set aside in a cool place to marinate while you prepare the rest of the salad.

Cut away the peel and pith from the grapefruit with a serrated knife. Hold the grapefruit in the palm of your hand and cut away each segment, working over a large bowl to catch the juices.

Add the olive oil to the grapefruit juice and whisk with a fork to combine. Add the grapefruit segments, cherry tomatoes, avocado, red onion and coriander to the bowl and toss to combine.

Divide the prepared salad between two serving plates. Remove the prawns from their marinade (using tongs or a slotted spoon) and arrange them on top. Drizzle the remaining marinade over the salad. Serve immediately with slices of warm garlic bread or similar.

400 g canned chickpeas, drained
and rinsed

100 g canned red kidney beans, drained
and rinsed

1 red onion, finely chopped

2 red chillies, deseeded and
finely chopped

2 tablespoons basil leaves, torn

1½ tablespoons chopped
flat leaf parsley

a small bunch of chives, finely chopped

250 g grilled chicken breast, chopped

250 g very ripe cherry tomatoes, halved

5 cm piece cucumber, chopped

fresh Parmesan cheese shavings

dressing

2 tablespoons extra virgin olive oil

4 tablespoons balsamic vinegar

2–3 garlic cloves, crushed

1 teaspoon wholegrain mustard

sea salt and freshly ground black pepper

serves 4

The great thing about this salad is you can eat it any time of the day, hot or cold. Because the beans hold their shape, it travels well, too. So if you make a bit too much for supper, just put it in an airtight container and take it with you the next day for lunch.

chicken and chilli
chickpea salad

To make the dressing, put the oil, vinegar, garlic and mustard in a salad bowl. Season with salt and pepper to taste, and stir to mix. Add the chickpeas, kidney beans, onion, chillies and herbs and mix well. Cover and chill in the refrigerator for 2–4 hours to let the flavours infuse.

When ready to eat, add the chicken, tomatoes and cucumber to the salad. Season with salt and pepper and toss well. Sprinkle with a few shavings of Parmesan. This is good served with warm pita bread.

20 uncooked tiger prawns

1 tablespoon sesame seeds

1 tablespoon chopped coriander

marinade

2.5 cm fresh ginger, peeled and grated

1–2 red chillies, deseeded and chopped

4 tablespoons freshly squeezed lime juice

1 tablespoon olive oil

2 tablespoons light soy sauce

½ teaspoon brown sugar

1–2 garlic cloves, crushed

mango salad

100 g bok choy, shredded

1 large ripe mango, peeled, stoned and chopped

75 g beansprouts

½ medium cucumber, chopped

1 red pepper, deseeded and thinly sliced

1 bunch spring onions, trimmed and chopped

freshly ground black pepper

serves 4

This salad is a really tasty, light supper and makes a great barbecue dish, too. You can replace the tiger prawns with monkfish, skinned, boned and cut into small pieces, if you want to ring the changes.

prawn and mango salad

Peel the prawns and, if necessary, remove and discard the thin black vein that runs down the back. Rinse and pat dry with kitchen paper. Put in a shallow dish.

To make the marinade, put the ginger, chillies, lime juice, olive oil, soy sauce, sugar and garlic in a bowl. Mix well. Pour the marinade over the prawns, stir, then cover. Refrigerate and let marinate for 15–30 minutes.

Meanwhile, prepare the salad. Put the bok choy and mango in a serving bowl. Add the beansprouts, cucumber, red pepper, spring onions and black pepper, to taste. Mix well and reserve.

Drain the prawns, reserving the marinade. Heat a non-stick frying pan or wok, add the prawns and cook, stirring frequently, for 2–3 minutes, or until pink. Add to the mango salad.

Pour the marinade into a small saucepan. Bring to the boil and boil for 2 minutes. Pour the marinade over the salad and toss lightly. Sprinkle with the sesame seeds and coriander and serve immediately.

This salad is very simple and you can also make it with cooked prawns. When preparing the lemongrass and kaffir lime leaves, make sure to chop them very finely indeed. If you can't find them, use a squeeze of lemon juice and some grated lime zest instead.

thai spicy prawn salad

Heat the oil in a wok, add the prawns and stir-fry for about 1 minute until opaque. Let cool.

Put the dressing ingredients in a large bowl and beat well with a fork until the sugar dissolves. Add the prawns and all the other ingredients, except the mint sprigs. Toss, then serve, topped with mint.

1 tablespoon peanut oil

12 uncooked prawns, shelled, deveined and halved lengthways

1 stalk lemongrass, very finely chopped

a handful of coriander leaves, finely chopped

2 pink Thai shallots or 1 small regular shallot, thinly sliced lengthways

3 spring onions, finely chopped

1 red chilli, deseeded and finely sliced

2 kaffir lime leaves, very finely chopped

12 cherry tomatoes, halved

a handful of mint sprigs, to serve

thai dressing

4 tablespoons Thai fish sauce

juice of 1 lemon or 2 limes

2 teaspoons brown sugar

2 tablespoons Thai red curry paste

serves 4

Poaching is a very healthy way of cooking the chicken in this salad: there is no added fat, and much of what's there melts away as the chicken cooks. This salad isn't authentic – that would involve stir-fried chicken mince – but it's easy and it tastes fresh and good, like most Vietnamese food. If you can't find Vietnamese mint, substitute ordinary mint, but you can't use ordinary basil instead of Asian basil – just leave it out.

vietnamese chicken salad
with chilli-lime dressing

Put the chicken in a wide saucepan, add the ginger, garlic, fish sauce, chilli and spring onions. Add chicken stock to cover and return to the boil. Reduce the heat, cover with a lid and simmer, without boiling, until the chicken is tender, about 15–20 minutes. Remove from the heat and let cool in the liquid. Remove from the liquid, take the meat off the bone, discard bone and skin, then pull the chicken into long shreds. Reserve the cooking liquid for another use, such as soup.

Put all the dressing ingredients in a screw-top jar and shake to mix.

To prepare the carrot, peel and shred into long matchsticks on a mandoline or the large blade of a box grater.

Pile the beansprouts on 4 plates. Add the carrot and chicken and top with the spring onions, mint and basil leaves, if using. Sprinkle with the dressing and roasted peanuts, then serve.

2 chicken breasts, on the bone

2.5 cm fresh ginger, peeled and sliced

1 garlic clove, crushed

1 tablespoon fish sauce or a pinch of salt

1 red chilli, sliced

2 spring onions, sliced

boiling chicken stock or water, to cover

1 young carrot

4 handfuls of beansprouts, rinsed and drained

6 spring onions, halved, then finely sliced lengthways

a handful of mint leaves, preferably Vietnamese mint

a handful of Asian basil leaves (optional)

2 tablespoons roasted peanuts, finely chopped

chilli-lime dressing

75 ml freshly squeezed lime juice, about 2–3 limes

1 tablespoon fish sauce

2 tablespoons brown sugar

1 green chilli, halved, deseeded and finely chopped

1 red chilli, halved, deseeded and finely chopped

1 garlic clove, crushed

2.5 cm fresh ginger, peeled and grated

serves 4

8 Chinese leaves
(Chinese or Napa cabbage)

1 large carrot

1 cucumber, about 20 cm long, halved, deseeded, cut into 5 cm sections, then thinly sliced lengthways

6 spring onions, sliced diagonally

8 slices dried mango, chopped

75 g cashews, toasted in a dry frying pan, then coarsely crushed

tamarind dressing

2 teaspoons tamarind paste

½ teaspoon Szechuan peppercorns, lightly toasted in a dry frying pan, then coarsely crushed

2 teaspoons sesame oil

1 garlic clove, finely chopped

½ teaspoon golden caster sugar or palm sugar, to taste

about 2 tablespoons chopped Thai basil, Vietnamese mint, or coriander

sea salt

serves 4

A simple vegetarian salad with fragrant South-east Asian flavours. It is versatile too, because other ingredients can be added according to the season. Sour tamarind and Szechuan pepper form an unusual partnership in the dressing – a combination of sour and hot.

vegetarian cashew salad
with tamarind dressing

First make the dressing. Mix the tamarind paste with 6 tablespoons warm water. Put it, the Szechuan pepper, sesame oil, garlic, sugar and chopped herbs in a screw-top jar and shake well. Set aside.

Stack the Chinese leaves on top of each other and slice them thinly. Grate the carrot into long sticks using the large blade of a box grater, or slice thinly into long strips. Divide the shredded leaves between 4 plates, add a layer of grated carrot, then the cucumber strips. Top with the spring onions and dried mango. Sprinkle the dressing over the salad, top with the cashews, then serve.

Variations Instead of Chinese leaves, use another crisp lettuce or Little Gem. For a non-vegetarian version, add 2 poached skinless chicken breasts, cooled and pulled into shreds, or 2 duck breasts, cooked in a stove-top grill pan, then sliced.

100 g green beans, trimmed

200 g finely shredded red or white cabbage

3 plum tomatoes, halved lengthways, deseeded and sliced

4 spring onions, sliced

4 cup-shaped lettuce leaves (optional)

50 g roasted peanuts, coarsely ground

dressing

a handful of coriander

2 red chillies, deseeded

2 garlic cloves, chopped

2 tablespoons light soy sauce

2 tablespoons freshly squeezed lime juice

2 tablespoons palm sugar or soft brown sugar

serves 4

This hybrid Thai coleslaw is based on the classic som tum, usually made from grated green papaya (when unripe, the fruit is firm, crunchy and perfect for grating). Green papaya is not the easiest ingredient to find, so red cabbage is used instead. The word 'coleslaw' comes from koolsla – Dutch for 'cabbage salad'. Here, these two classic dishes become a salad with a delicious new twist.

thai coleslaw

To make the dressing, reserve a few coriander leaves, then put the rest in a blender or food processor. Add the chillies, garlic, soy sauce, lime juice and sugar and blend until smooth. Set aside.

Blanch the beans in boiling water for 2 minutes, then refresh in cold water. Mix the cabbage, beans, tomatoes and spring onions in a bowl. Pour the dressing on top, toss well to coat and let marinate for about 30 minutes. Spoon into bowls lined with the lettuce leaves, if using, sprinkle with the ground peanuts and the reserved coriander leaves, then serve.

You can alter the vegetables in this salad according to what's in season. Try broccoli or carrots sliced lengthways into matchsticks, spinach leaves, sliced Chinese cabbage or cauliflower florets. Snake beans keep their crunch better than ordinary beans, so are good for this salad.

indonesian gado-gado

To make the peanut sauce, toast the peanuts in a dry frying pan. Transfer to a tea towel, rub off any skins, then put the nuts in a blender. Grind to a coarse meal, then add the chillies, onion, garlic, salt, sugar and coconut milk. Blend to a purée, then transfer to a saucepan and cook, stirring, until thickened.

Thinly slice the halved cucumbers diagonally, put on a plate, sprinkle with salt, let stand for 10 minutes, then rinse and pat dry with kitchen paper. Chill.

Cook the snake beans in boiling salted water until al dente, then drain, rinse immediately under cold running water, and transfer to a bowl of iced water. Just before serving, drain again and pat dry with kitchen paper.

Peel the pepper with a vegetable peeler, cut off and discard the top and bottom, then halve, deseed and thinly slice lengthways.

Heat 2 tablespoons peanut oil in a frying pan, add the tofu and cook until brown on both sides, then drain and slice thickly.

To cook the prawn crackers, fill a wok one-third full with peanut oil and heat to 190°C (375°F). Drop in one cracker to test the temperature – it should puff up immediately. Add the crackers, crowding them so they curl up, then cook until puffed and golden, about 3 seconds. Remove and drain on kitchen paper.

To cook the onion rings, reheat the oil, add the sliced onion and deep-fry until crisp and golden. Remove and drain on kitchen paper.

Arrange the cucumbers, snake beans, pepper, tofu, beansprouts, lettuce, daikon and quartered eggs on a large platter. Top with the onion rings and crackers, drizzle with the peanut sauce, sprinkle with salt and serve.

2 mini cucumbers, such as Lebanese, halved lengthways and deseeded

8 snake beans, cut into 5 cm lengths

1 orange or red pepper

peanut oil, for frying

2 firm tofu cakes

20–25 prawn crackers

2 onions, thinly sliced into rings

a large handful of beansprouts, rinsed, drained and trimmed

2 heads Little Gem lettuce

15 cm daikon (white radish or mooli), peeled and grated

2 hard-boiled eggs, quartered

sea salt flakes

peanut sauce

250 g shelled fresh peanuts

2 red chillies, halved, deseeded and finely chopped

2 bird's eye chillies, halved, deseeded and finely chopped

1 onion, finely chopped

1 garlic clove, crushed

1 teaspoon sea salt

2 teaspoons brown sugar

200 ml canned coconut milk

serves 4

1 litre canned coconut milk

250 g somen or cellophane noodles

4 tablespoons peanut oil

500 g boneless chicken, cut in 1 cm strips

1 small packet beansprouts, trimmed

4 spring onions, sliced diagonally

1 red chilli, deseeded and finely sliced

sea salt

sprigs of mint and coriander, to serve

spice paste

4 red or orange chillies (not habañeros)

3 stalks lemongrass, finely sliced

2.5 cm fresh galangal or ginger, sliced

1 teaspoon ground turmeric

4 candlenuts or 8 almonds, crushed

1 teaspoon shrimp paste*

1 garlic clove, chopped

4 shallots or 2 mild onions, sliced

1 tablespoon coriander seeds

serves 4

Laksas are one-bowl meals from Malaysia and Singapore. The spice paste usually contains candlenuts, but if you can't find any, use almonds or macadamias instead.

singapore coconut laksa

Open the cans of coconut milk and pour the thick and thin bits into separate bowls. Put all the spice paste ingredients into a spice grinder or clean coffee grinder and work to a mush, in batches if necessary.

If using somen noodles, cook in boiling salted water for 2½–3 minutes. Add a splash of cold water from time to time, then return to the boil. If using cellophane noodles, soak in hot water for 15 minutes, then boil for 1 minute before serving.

Heat the oil in a wok, add the chicken and stir-fry until lightly golden and cooked through. Remove from the wok and set aside. Add the spice paste and cook, stirring, until aromatic – about 6–8 minutes.

Add the thin coconut milk, bring to the boil, stirring, add the cooked chicken and return to the boil, still stirring. Add the thick part of the coconut milk, beansprouts, spring onions, chilli and salt to taste and cook gently, stirring, until well heated (keep stirring or the coconut milk will curdle).

Serve in large soup bowls with sprigs of mint and coriander.

*Note Shrimp paste (blachan) is sold by Asian grocers, and must be either covered and zapped in a microwave before use, or wrapped in foil and grilled for a few minutes. If you can't find shrimp paste, use a similar quantity of Thai fish sauce or anchovy essence.

The spice paste in this recipe can be made in quantity and frozen – a useful standby. You can use a ready-made Thai curry paste to save time, if you like. The tamarind gives this laksa a lemony taste.

tamarind fish laksa

If using dried noodles, cook in boiling salted water for 10–12 minutes: if fresh, boil for 2–2½ minutes. During boiling, add a splash of cold water once or twice during the cooking time, then return to the boil. Drain and cover with cold water until ready to assemble the dish.

Put all the spice paste ingredients, except the peanut oil, in a blender or spice grinder and blend to a purée, adding a few tablespoons of water as necessary to make a paste. Heat the oil in a wok, add the paste and stir-fry for about 6 minutes until the rawness is cooked out of the spices.

Add the stock and ginger and heat until boiling, add the fish, turn off the heat and put on the lid. Leave for about 5 minutes until the fish is cooked, then break the fish into large pieces in the stock. Reheat to boiling point, then stir in the tamarind paste, sugar, salt and pepper.

Drain the noodles, then dunk them and the prawns, if using, into boiling water until heated through. Drain, then put a pile of the hot noodles in 4 large Chinese soup bowls, ladle the fish and stock over the top and sprinkle with prawns, mint, beansprouts, coriander and chillies.

500 g fresh udon noodles, or 250 g dried

1 litre fish stock or water

2.5 cm fresh ginger or galangal, peeled and grated

500 g skinless, boneless fish fillets

1 tablespoon tamarind paste or freshly squeezed juice of 1 lime

1 teaspoon brown sugar or palm sugar

sea salt and freshly ground black pepper, to taste

spice paste

3 dried chillies, deseeded and soaked

2 stalks lemongrass, chopped

2.5 cm fresh ginger or galangal, peeled and grated

1 teaspoon ground turmeric

1 tablespoon shrimp paste (see note page 77)

12 spring onions, finely sliced

1 tablespoon peanut oil

to serve

8–12 cooked, peeled medium prawns (optional)

1 bunch Vietnamese mint or mint

1 small packet beansprouts, trimmed

1 bunch coriander leaves, torn

2 red chillies, deseeded and thinly sliced

serves 4

fish and seafood

This fast, flavoursome supper is ideal for serving to friends as a light main course. If you want to reduce preparation time further, you can use two 350 g packs of any prepared stir-fry vegetables – such as red peppers, beansprouts and courgettes – instead of the leeks, carrots and onion.

chilli scallops with leeks
and lime crème fraîche

First make the lime crème fraiche. Put the crème fraîche in a small bowl, add the chopped coriander and grated lime zest and juice and season with salt and pepper. Set aside.

Heat 1 tablespoon of the oil in a large non-stick frying pan or wok and stir-fry the bacon lardons until golden. Remove from the pan with a slotted spoon, drain and set aside on kitchen paper. In the remaining fat, stir-fry the leeks, carrots, onion, chillies and garlic until soft and golden brown. Add the honey and soy sauce, transfer to a bowl or plate and keep warm.

Rinse the pan under running water and wipe dry. Add the remaining oil and heat until scorching hot. Season the scallops with pepper and fry briefly on both sides in the pan, allowing around 1½ minutes on each side; they should be firm-textured after cooking. Remove from the pan once they are cooked and keep warm.

Return the vegetable mixture and bacon lardons to the pan and reheat until piping hot. Divide the vegetables between 4 serving plates, top with 4 scallops per plate and add a generous spoonful of the lime crème fraîche. Garnish each with a coriander sprig and serve immediately.

2 tablespoons sunflower oil

50 g bacon lardons

2 large leeks, trimmed and cut into strips

100 g carrots, peeled and cut into strips

1 large onion, thinly sliced

2 red chillies, deseeded and finely chopped

2 garlic cloves, crushed

2 tablespoons runny honey

2 tablespoons soy sauce

16 large scallops, prepared with coral attached

sea salt and freshly ground black pepper

lime crème fraîche

175 ml crème fraîche

2 tablespoons chopped coriander, plus extra sprigs to garnish

finely grated zest of 1 lime

1 tablespoon freshly squeezed lime juice

serves 4

1 tablespoon olive oil

200 g basmati rice

1 large onion, chopped

1 teaspoon ground turmeric

400 g canned chopped tomatoes

1 large red pepper, deseeded
and finely chopped

1–2 garlic cloves, chopped

500 ml chicken stock

400 g canned butter beans, drained
and rinsed

1–2 red chillies, deseeded and
thinly sliced

500 g cooked peeled prawns, thawed
if frozen

3 tablespoons coriander,
coarsely chopped

sea salt and freshly ground black pepper

serves 4

This makes a great midweek supper dish, and it is an easy way to increase your vegetable intake by adding vegetables of your choice. Try throwing in some freezer staples such as frozen peas, corn kernels or green beans. They cook in minutes and don't require any preparation.

prawn and butter bean rice

Heat the oil in a large non-stick saucepan. Add the rice, onion and turmeric and cook over medium heat, stirring, for 2 minutes. Add the tomatoes, pepper, garlic, stock and salt and pepper, to taste. Cover the pan with a tight-fitting lid, reduce the heat and simmer for 15 minutes, until most of the stock has been absorbed by the rice.

Add the butter beans, chillies and prawns to the rice mixture and stir through gently. Replace the lid and cook for a further 3 minutes, or until the stock is absorbed and the prawns are thoroughly warmed through. Stir in the coriander and serve immediately.

Variation Brown four skinned, boneless chicken thighs then add to the rice and onion and proceed as above. Add some frozen peas and corn kernels with the butter beans and prawns and cook for 3–5 minutes or until cooked and piping hot. Serve with lemon wedges, if you like.

Salmon cutlets and plenty of fresh vegetables make this a delicious, healthy meal. As a variation, exchange the leeks for thinly sliced courgettes and add some sugar snap peas and tiny broccoli florets. If you like, try using oyster or fresh shiitake mushrooms and add some shredded Chinese cabbage leaves or bok choy.

asian salmon
with rice noodles

Wash the salmon cutlets and pat dry with kitchen paper. Rub the five spice powder into both sides of the fish and season well with black pepper. Set aside for 30 minutes.

Meanwhile, put the noodles in a bowl, cover with boiling water and let soak for 15 minutes. Drain, then add the noodles to a saucepan of boiling water and cook for 1 minute. Drain and keep the noodles warm.

Cook the salmon cutlets under a preheated hot grill for 7–10 minutes, or until thoroughly cooked, turning once halfway through the cooking time.

Heat a non-stick frying pan. Add the soy sauce, honey, ginger, garlic, carrot and leek to the pan and sauté the vegetables for 3–4 minutes, until beginning to soften. Add the mushrooms and sauté for a further 2 minutes.

Divide the noodles between 4 bowls or plates. Spoon the vegetables and their juices over the noodles and put the grilled salmon on top. Sprinkle with coriander, if using, and serve.

4 salmon cutlets, about 115 g each

2 teaspoons Chinese five-spice powder

300 g rice vermicelli noodles

2 tablespoons light soy sauce

2 teaspoons clear honey

2.5 cm fresh ginger, peeled and grated

2 garlic cloves, crushed

1 large carrot, thinly sliced

1 large leek, sliced

350 g mushrooms, wiped and sliced

1 tablespoon chopped coriander (optional)

freshly ground black pepper

serves 4

If you have friends coming round for a midweek supper and you need to make something special but don't want to spend more than 10 minutes in the kitchen, this recipe is the answer. Any other seafood or shellfish, such as baby squid, would also work well in this recipe.

chilli scallops with spaghetti

Rinse the scallops in cold water and discard the black vein, if necessary. Pat dry on kitchen paper. If the scallops are large, cut them into 2 or 3 slices.

Bring a large saucepan of water to the boil. Add a pinch of salt, then the spaghetti, and cook until al dente or according to the instructions on the packet. Drain the pasta, reserving 2 tablespoons of the cooking water. Return the pasta and the reserved cooking water to the warm pan.

Put the garlic, chillies and coriander in a small bowl and mix. Heat a heavy-based frying pan and add 1 tablespoon olive oil. Add the chilli mixture to the pan and cook for 1 minute, stirring, then add the scallops. Stir well until coated with the oil and chillies. Cook, stirring occasionally, for 2–3 minutes, until the scallops are cooked. Season to taste and keep warm in a low oven.

Add the cream and remaining oil to the spaghetti and heat gently, stirring frequently, until piping hot. Serve immediately, topped with the scallops.

16–24 scallops

500 g spaghetti

4 garlic cloves, coarsely chopped

1–2 red chillies, deseeded and coarsely chopped

1 tablespoon chopped coriander

2 tablespoons extra virgin olive oil

120 ml half-fat single cream

sea salt and freshly ground black pepper

serves 4

4 tuna steaks, about 175 g each

2–3 garlic cloves, crushed

1 teaspoon ground cumin

2 teaspoons finely grated lime zest

1 tablespoon freshly squeezed lime juice

2 teaspoons olive oil

1 teaspoon ground coriander

freshly ground black pepper

pepper noodles

225 g egg noodles

1 teaspoon sunflower oil

1 garlic clove, chopped

1 red pepper, deseeded and thinly sliced

1 yellow pepper, deseeded and thinly sliced

finely grated zest and juice of 1 lime

1 tablespoon light soy sauce

sea salt and freshly ground black pepper

to serve

1 red pepper, deseeded and chopped

2 tablespoons chopped coriander

4 lime wedges

serves 4

Fresh tuna, unlike canned tuna, is a good source of those all-important omega-3 fatty acids, which help to protect against heart disease. Don't overcook the tuna because it can become quite dry and chewy. Fresh tuna is at its most tender when it is still pink in the middle.

spicy tuna steaks
with pepper noodles

Wipe the tuna or lightly rinse and pat dry with kitchen paper. Put the garlic, cumin, lime zest, lime juice, oil, ground coriander and black pepper in a small bowl. Mix to make a paste. Spread the paste thinly on both sides of the tuna steaks and leave to marinate for at least 15 minutes.

Heat a non-stick frying pan until hot and press the tuna steaks into the pan to seal them. Lower the heat and cook for 3 minutes. Turn the fish over and cook for a further 3–5 minutes, until cooked to personal preference. Remove from the pan, transfer to a plate and keep warm in a low oven.

To make the pepper noodles, bring a large saucepan of water to the boil. Add the noodles and cook for 4 minutes, or according to the timings on the packet. Drain, rinse and reserve. Heat a non-stick frying pan, add the oil, garlic and peppers and sauté gently, until the vegetables start to soften. Add the drained noodles, the lime zest and juice and soy sauce. Cook for 1–2 minutes, turning frequently, until warmed through.

Transfer the noodles to warm serving plates and top with the tuna steaks. Sprinkle with some chopped red pepper and coriander. Add a wedge of lime and serve immediately.

Variation Try a different marinade for the tuna: blend 2 crushed garlic cloves with 1 deseeded and finely chopped chilli, 2 teaspoons of freshly grated ginger, 2 tablespoons of chopped fresh coriander, 1 teaspoon of Thai fish sauce and 1 tablespoon of olive oil. Marinate as above.

Use the large, dried red New Mexico chillies if you can get them. They are available in specialist shops and by mail order. Alternatively, substitute one small dried red chilli (much hotter than the New Mexico version). Mussels are naturally salty, so take care when seasoning this recipe. This is good served with toasted sourdough bread.

steamed mussels
in a red chilli broth

2 garlic cloves

4 red tomatoes, sliced

2 dried red New Mexico chillies, stemmed and deseeded

300 ml fish stock

2 tablespoons olive oil

1 kg mussels, scrubbed and debearded

150 ml single cream (optional)

salt and freshly ground black pepper

ground paprika, to serve

serves 4

Roast the garlic and tomatoes in a preheated oven at 150°C (300°F) Gas Mark 2 for 1 hour.

To make the broth, soak the chillies in the stock and 150 ml water for about 1 hour until softened and limp. Purée in a blender and set aside.

Heat 1 tablespoon of the olive oil in a pan and sauté the garlic and tomato until reheated. Add the mussels, stir in the broth, cover and steam for about 5–7 minutes until the mussels have opened. Discard any that remain closed. Taste and adjust the seasoning, then stir in the cream, if using, and serve immediately with a sprinkling of ground paprika.

300 ml canned coconut milk

1 red chilli, deseeded and sliced

1 green chilli, deseeded and sliced

2 stalks of lemongrass, cut in half lengthways

500 g mussels, scrubbed and debearded

500 g cod or monkfish tail

500 g uncooked tiger prawns, shelled and deveined

leaves from 1 bunch of coriander, torn

serves 4

Thai fish curries taste clean and fresh, and are absolutely packed with spicy flavour. It's important not to overcook the seafood, so remove it from the broth as soon as it is cooked, then reheat just before serving.

thai seafood curry
with coriander and coconut milk

Pour the coconut milk into a pan, add the chillies and lemongrass and bring to the boil. Add the mussels and remove as soon as they open. Add the cod and tiger prawns and poach gently until the prawns change colour and the fish becomes opaque.

Remove the fish and prawns from the pan and set aside with the mussels. Gently pull the cod into bite-sized pieces.

Return the coconut milk to the boil and reduce by half. Return the seafood to the pan and reheat, then serve scattered with torn coriander leaves and accompanied by fragrant Thai rice or pasta.

You can adapt this recipe for the barbecue – the woodsmoke adds a marvellous depth of flavour. Always cook the prawns with their shells on, again for extra flavour.

prawn brochettes
with chilli, papaya and mango salsa

To make the salsa, mix the ingredients together in a small container, cover and chill for up to 6 hours.

Put the prawns in a bowl and sprinkle over the chilli oil and the lime juice. Marinate for 1–2 hours.

Thread a wedge of red onion onto each skewer, then thread on the prawns, followed by a slice of lime. Brush with the marinade, sprinkle with sea salt, then cook under a preheated grill or on the barbecue for a few minutes on each side.

Serve, garnished with wedges of lime and onion, the sliced chilli and torn coriander leaves, together with the salsa spooned over or served separately. Rice, pita bread or salad would be suitable accompaniments.

24 uncooked, unshelled prawns

1 teaspoon chilli oil

freshly squeezed juice of 2 limes, plus 1 lime, sliced, and 1 lime, quartered

1 large red onion, cut into 8 wedges

sea salt

chilli, papaya and mango salsa

1 large ripe mango, peeled, stoned and diced

1 ripe papaya, about 250 g, peeled, deseeded and diced

1 tablespoon balsamic vinegar

1 tablespoon chopped red chillies

salt and freshly ground black pepper

to serve

1 red chilli, sliced

coriander leaves

4 wooden skewers, soaked in water for at least 30 minutes

serves 4

The piri piri is a fiercely hot chilli introduced to Africa by the Portuguese. The name is also used for the hot sauces in which the pods are used. Versions of piri piri sauce can be found from Mozambique and Angola to Brazil, as well as in Portugal itself. For this recipe, use any hot, thin red chillies. Nigella seeds are not a traditional component of piri piri recipes, but they add a special flavour and texture.

african seafood kebabs
with piri piri basting oil

To make the piri piri basting oil, put the garlic, chillies, lemon juice and olive oil into a blender and blend until smooth. Transfer to a bowl and stir in the nigella seeds, if using.

Dip the prawns and scallops into the basting oil and coat well. Thread the prawns and scallops alternately onto the skewers, with the bay leaves between them.

Set apart on a grill rack over a grill tray. Cook at high heat under a preheated grill for about 5 minutes or until done, turning once during cooking. (Don't overcook or the scallops will be tough – prawns and scallops are done when the flesh becomes opaque.) Brush with the piri piri basting oil several times while the skewers are cooking. Alternatively, put the remaining oil into a small saucepan, boil for 1–2 minutes, then serve as a dipping sauce. Serve the kebabs with ciabatta or focaccia bread.

12 large uncooked prawns, peeled, but with tail fins intact

8 large or 12 small scallops, trimmed

12–20 bay leaves

piri piri basting oil

3 garlic cloves, crushed

5–6 red bird's eye chillies or 8–9 regular red chillies, deseeded and coarsely chopped

freshly squeezed juice of ½ lemon

100 ml extra virgin olive oil

½ teaspoon nigella seeds (optional)

4 metal skewers

serves 4

Chermoula is a spicy Moroccan sauce or marinade for fish. In Tangier, huge baskets of spices and herbs, such as the coriander and cumin for chermoula, are lined up for sale in the souks. The colour of this sauce is produced by fresh coriander, while the chilli powder gives it a kick. It can be used as both a marinade and a topping.

moroccan grilled fish
with chermoula spice paste

To make the chermoula, put the coriander and garlic into a blender or food processor. Add the pimentón, cumin, chilli powder, olive oil, lemon juice and a pinch of salt and blend to a smooth paste – if necessary, add a dash of water to let the blades run. Alternatively, use a mortar and pestle.

About 30 minutes before cooking the fish, sprinkle it with salt, put a spoonful of chermoula onto each steak and rub all over. Set aside to marinate.

When ready to cook, brush a stove-top grill pan with olive oil and heat over medium-high heat until very hot. Add the fish to the pan and cook for 1–2 minutes, depending on thickness. Don't move the fish until it loosens and will move without sticking. Turn it over and continue cooking for 1–2 minutes more. If the fish is very thick, cook for 1 minute longer, but do not overcook or the flesh will be tough. (If you have a small pan, cook in batches of 1 or 2 and keep them warm in a very low oven while you cook the remainder.)

To serve, top each fish steak with the remaining chermoula and extra coriander.

If you would like to serve the fish with typical North African accompaniments, roast some butternut squash or sweet potatoes with olive oil and cinnamon, and soak some couscous with a little saffron added to the water.

4 tuna, marlin or swordfish steaks, about 200 g each, lightly scored

sea salt

olive oil, for grilling

coriander leaves, to serve

chermoula

a few handfuls of coriander leaves and stems, coarsely chopped

3 garlic cloves, chopped

¼ teaspoon sweet pimentón (Spanish oak-smoked paprika)

½ teaspoon ground cumin

½ teaspoon chilli powder

4 tablespoons extra virgin olive oil

freshly squeezed juice of ½ lemon

sea salt

a stove-top grill pan

serves 4

2 garlic cloves, chopped

3 cm fresh ginger, peeled and chopped

3 tablespoons sunflower or peanut oil

4 small tomatoes, skinned and chopped

2 teaspoons white vinegar (wine or malt)

500 g uncooked shelled tiger prawns

a few curry leaves*

a few red chillies, deseeded and sliced

sea salt

freshly shaved coconut, to serve

masala paste

1 small onion, quartered

grated flesh of ½ coconut,
fresh or frozen

2 black peppercorns

2 red chillies, deseeded

¼ teaspoon ground turmeric

2 teaspoons ground coriander

½ teaspoon black mustard seeds

serves 4

A recipe from Kerala, the long and fertile state in India's south-west. Kerala, like most of South India, reveres the coconut, so this prawn and coconut recipe is a good example of its fine seafood dishes. Rice and pooris (South Indian breads) are delicious served with this dish.

coconut prawn masala

Put all the masala ingredients in a blender and work into a thick paste, adding a dash of water if necessary to let the blades run. Remove and set aside.

Put the garlic and ginger into the clean blender and grind to a paste. Alternatively, use a mortar and pestle.

Heat 2 tablespoons oil in a wok or frying pan. Add the garlic and ginger paste and fry for a few seconds. Add the masala paste and stir-fry until the paste leaves the sides of the pan, about 8–10 minutes. Add the chopped tomatoes, vinegar, salt and 250 ml water. Bring to the boil, add the prawns, reduce the heat and cook for 2–3 minutes, until the prawns turn pink. Transfer to a serving bowl.

Heat the remaining oil in a small pan, add the curry leaves and red chillies and fry for about 45 seconds or so (this is called 'tempering'). Pour the tempered curry leaves and chillies over the prawns, top with shaved coconut and serve.

*Note Curry leaves are best fresh, and are often available in Indian or South-east Asian markets. Fresh ones may be frozen. If necessary, dried ones may be used instead. (Note that curry leaves are not related to the grey curry plant grown in some herb gardens.)

This is similar to the popular dish Pad Thai, but drier, less sweet and omits certain key ingredients such as eggs, substituting stir-fry vegetables instead. Tiny, blindingly hot bird's eye chillies are an essential spice in South-east Asian cuisine: if you prefer less heat, use another kind of chilli or reduce the number.

stir-fried peanut prawns
with coriander noodles

Put the noodles into a bowl and cover with boiling water. Let soak for 4 minutes or according to the instructions on the packet. Drain, return to the bowl and cover with cold water until ready to serve. Have a kettle of boiling water ready to reheat.

Put 3 tablespoons of the oil into a non-stick wok, heat well and swirl to coat. Add the ground coriander, kaffir lime leaves, lemongrass, red chillies and chopped spring onions and stir-fry briefly. Add the garlic and stir-fry again for 20 seconds. Add the prepared vegetables, sugar and 2 tablespoons of the fish sauce and stir-fry over medium-high heat for 1 minute.

Add the prawns and lemon juice and stir-fry for 1 minute, then add half the ground peanuts. Mix well, add the remaining tablespoon of fish sauce and cook for 2 more minutes or until the prawns turn pink.

Meanwhile, drain the noodles again and return them to the bowl. Cover with boiling water, drain and return to the bowl. Add 2 tablespoons peanut oil, toss to coat, add the coriander and toss again. Add the noodles to the wok, toss to coat, then serve immediately topped with coriander, green chillies, spring onions, beansprouts and the remaining peanuts.

*Note You can also substitute your own choice of vegetables, such as broccoli and cauliflower florets, red pepper strips, asparagus tips, sliced onion, sugar snap peas or string beans, all cut into bite-sized pieces.

150 g rice stick noodles

5 tablespoons peanut oil

a pinch of ground coriander

2 kaffir lime leaves, 1 finely sliced or crushed and 1 left whole

1 stalk of lemongrass, very finely chopped

3–4 red bird's eye chillies, deseeded and thinly sliced

3 spring onions, chopped

1 fat garlic clove, crushed

100 g ready-mixed stir-fry vegetables, without beansprouts*

a pinch of sugar

3 tablespoons Thai fish sauce

250 g uncooked, shelled tiger prawns, deveined (about 400 g, shell-on)

freshly squeezed juice of 1 lemon

150 g dry-roasted peanuts, coarsely ground

25 g fresh coriander, finely chopped

to serve

a handful of coriander leaves, chopped

a few green bird's eye chillies, deseeded and finely sliced

2 spring onions, green part only, finely sliced

a handful of beansprouts

serves 4

500 g firm fish such as salmon, monkfish or cod

1 tablespoon ground turmeric

1 teaspoon salt

100 g ghee (clarified butter), butter or sunflower oil

1 onion, chopped

1 garlic clove, crushed

2 small green chillies, deseeded if preferred, and chopped

3 cm fresh ginger, peeled and grated

12 cardamom pods, crushed

6 cloves, crushed

1 cinnamon stick, about 5 cm

500 ml canned coconut milk

freshly squeezed lemon juice, to taste

torn coriander leaves, to serve

serves 4

A mollee is a South Indian sauce, one of those dishes known wrongly in the rest of the world as a 'curry'. It is mostly used for poaching fish, but is also delicious as a medium for reheating cooked meats or vegetables. The first step is to make the sauce: after that, you may add what you like. In the south of India, this is often served with great mounds of fluffy rice flavoured with cumin seed.

fish mollee

Cut the fish into 3 cm strips. Mix the turmeric and salt on a plate, roll the fish in the mixture and set aside for a few minutes.

Meanwhile, heat the ghee, butter or oil in a flameproof casserole or large saucepan. Add the onion, garlic, chillies, ginger, cardamom, cloves and cinnamon stick and sauté until the onion is softened and translucent.

Add the coconut milk, heat until simmering and cook until the mixture is quite thick. Add the fish to the casserole, then spoon the sauce over the top, making sure the fish is well covered. Cook for 10 minutes on top of the stove or in a preheated oven at 150°C (300°F) Gas 2, until the fish is opaque all the way through. Serve sprinkled with lemon juice and coriander.

Kerala, on the south-west coast of India, is coconut country – and one of the great spice-producing areas of the world (it was famous as such even in ancient times). The region has an inspired touch with seafood.

kerala coconut chilli prawns

Bring a large saucepan of water to the boil and plunge in the spinach for 20 seconds. Remove with a slotted spoon and refresh under cold running water to stop the cooking process; squeeze out as much water as possible. Set aside. Add the beans and cook just until crunchy, about 3 minutes. Drain, refresh in cold water, drain again and add to the spinach.

Preheat the oven to 150°C (300°F) Gas 2. Heat the ghee or oil in an ovenproof casserole, add the onion, garlic, ginger and chillies and fry until soft. Add the cumin, pepper, cardamom, cloves, salt and 1 teaspoon of the lemon juice and cook for 5 minutes.

Stir in the coconut milk. Add the beans and prawns, then stir in the chopped coriander and the rest of the lemon juice. Cook in the preheated oven for about 25 minutes, or until the prawns have just become opaque. Add the spinach for the last 5 minutes to reheat. Do not overcook or the prawns will be tough.

Sprinkle with the sliced green chillies and a handful of coriander leaves if you like, then serve with plain rice or rice mixed with pan-toasted cumin seeds.

250 g spinach, well washed

100 g green beans

50 g ghee (clarified butter) or peanut oil

2 onions, chopped

3 garlic cloves, chopped

3 cm fresh ginger, peeled and chopped

2 green chillies, deseeded and chopped

1 tablespoon ground cumin

1 teaspoon freshly ground black pepper

6 green cardamom pods, crushed

2 cloves

a pinch of salt

freshly squeezed juice of ½ lemon

500 ml thick coconut milk

500 g uncooked prawns, shelled and deveined

3 tablespoons chopped coriander

to serve (optional)

3–4 green chillies, sliced

a handful of coriander leaves

serves 4

1 tablespoon peanut oil

400 ml canned coconut milk

750 g firm fish fillets, such as monkfish, cod or John Dory

spice paste

1 onion, sliced

3 garlic cloves, chopped

6 small hot green chillies, deseeded and sliced

5 cm fresh ginger, peeled and sliced

1 teaspoon ground white pepper

1 teaspoon ground coriander

$\frac{1}{2}$ teaspoon ground turmeric

$\frac{1}{2}$ teaspoon ground cumin

1 teaspoon shrimp paste (see note page 77)

1 tablespoon Thai fish sauce

1 stalk of lemongrass, peeled and finely sliced

to serve

sprigs of Thai basil (optional)*

2 limes, halved

serves 4

Thai curries are easy to make, quick to cook and totally delicious. The secret is in the mixture of spices and the freshness of the paste. Here the paste is made in a food processor using ground spices but, if you prefer using whole ones, break them down in a coffee grinder kept solely for that purpose.

thai green fish curry

Put all the spice paste ingredients in a food processor and work them into a fine purée. Alternatively, use a mortar and pestle. Set aside.

Put the oil in a wok and heat well. Add the spice paste and stir-fry for a few seconds to release the aromas. Add the thick portion from the top of the coconut milk, stir well and boil to thicken a little.

Add the fish and turn the pieces over in the sauce until well coated. Reheat to simmering and cook just until they start to become opaque, about 2 minutes.

Add the remaining coconut milk and continue cooking until the fish is cooked through. Serve topped with Thai basil, if using, plus the halved limes and some fragrant Thai rice or noodles.

*Note Thai and Vietnamese basil is quite different from ordinary basil. It is sold in Asian food markets – omit it if you can't find it.

½ tablespoon grated fresh ginger

2 tablespoons chopped coriander

1 teaspoon ground cumin

1 teaspoon ground coriander

1 tablespoon freshly squeezed lemon juice

4 skinless salmon fillets, 125 g each

1 teaspoon sunflower oil

sea salt and freshly ground
black pepper

dhal

150 g red lentils, rinsed

1 onion, finely chopped

1 tablespoon grated fresh ginger

½ teaspoon ground turmeric

2 garlic cloves, sliced

1 teaspoon cumin seeds

½ teaspoon black mustard seeds

2 teaspoons sunflower oil

410 g canned chickpeas, drained
and rinsed

3 tomatoes, deseeded and chopped

75 g spinach leaves, rinsed

1 tablespoon freshly squeezed
lemon juice

serves 4

A delicious dish fusing Indian dhal and spices with seared salmon, packed with health-enhancing fish oils. It's a complete meal in one and doesn't need anything else to accompany it.

spiced salmon
with chickpea dhal

Start by making the spice paste for the salmon. In a bowl, mix the ginger with the coriander, spices, lemon juice and seasoning, then rub into the salmon fillets. Cover and set aside at room temperature to allow the flavours to develop while making the dhal.

Put the lentils in a saucepan with the onion, ginger, turmeric and 500 ml water and cook, covered, for 15 minutes until the lentils start to break up.

Fry the garlic, cumin seeds and black mustard seeds in the sunflower oil in a frying pan until the garlic is golden and the seeds begin to pop. Quickly stir into the lentils, followed by the chickpeas. Simmer for 3 minutes.

Heat a non-stick frying pan and drizzle the sunflower oil over the salmon fillets. Pan fry the salmon for 3 minutes on each side until the spice crust is golden and the salmon is just cooked through, but still moist.

Stir the tomatoes, spinach and lemon juice into the dhal until the spinach has just wilted. Add seasoning to taste, then ladle the dhal onto deep plates. Place the salmon on top of the dhal to serve.

This quick curry will fill your kitchen with a wonderful aroma as it cooks. The many spices give a complex flavour to a sauce that is made in a matter of minutes.

goan prawn curry

Mix the spices to a paste with a little water in a saucepan. Stir in the garlic, ginger and 400 ml cold water, add seasoning and bring to the boil. Simmer for 10 minutes until the sauce has slightly reduced and the raw flavour of the spices is released.

Meanwhile, cook the green beans in a separate saucepan of lightly salted boiling water for about 5 minutes or until tender, then drain.

Stir the tamarind paste and creamed coconut into the spicy sauce base until smooth. Add the prawns and cook for about 2 minutes or until they turn pink. Stir in the green beans and spinach and cook briefly until the spinach has wilted. Ladle the curry into bowls and serve with basmati rice or chapattis.

1 tablespoon ground coriander

½ tablespoon paprika

1 teaspoon ground cumin

½ teaspoon cayenne or hot chilli powder

½ teaspoon ground turmeric

3 garlic cloves, crushed

2 teaspoons grated fresh ginger

250 g green beans, halved

1 tablespoon tamarind paste or freshly squeezed lemon juice

25 g creamed coconut, grated

400 g uncooked tiger prawns, shelled and deveined

100 g young leaf spinach, rinsed

sea salt and freshly ground black pepper

serves 4

Green curry is a staple dish of Thailand. The green curry paste here will make 6–10 tablespoons of paste. Freeze the leftovers in ice cube trays, then decant the cubes into a freezer bag. Each cube will give about 1 tablespoon paste.

green curry with prawns

First make the green curry paste. Using a mortar and pestle, grind all the ingredients to a thick paste.

Heat the oil in a large saucepan, add the garlic and fry until golden brown. Stir in 2 tablespoons of the green curry paste, mixing well. Add the prawns and stir-fry until just cooked through. Add the coconut cream and bring to the boil, stirring constantly. Add the stock. Return to the boil, stirring constantly.

Keeping the curry simmering, add the chillies, fish sauce, aubergines and sugar and simmer until the aubergines are cooked but still crunchy (do not overcook or the prawns will be tough).

Stir in the basil leaves just before pouring into the serving bowl. Serve with rice and other Thai dishes.

2 tablespoons peanut or sunflower oil

2 garlic cloves, finely chopped

12 uncooked king prawns, shelled and deveined

600 ml coconut cream

600 ml vegetable stock

2 large red chillies, sliced diagonally into thin ovals

4 tablespoons Thai fish sauce

8 round green Thai aubergines, quartered, or 1 Chinese eggplant, cut into 1 cm slices

1 tablespoon sugar

30 fresh sweet basil leaves

green curry paste

1 teaspoon coriander seeds

1 teaspoon cumin seeds

1 teaspoon white peppercorns

1 tablespoon chopped lemongrass

3 cm fresh galangal or ginger, peeled and chopped

2 long green chillies, chopped

10 small green chillies, chopped

2 tablespoons chopped garlic

3 pink Thai shallots or 2 regular ones, chopped

3 coriander roots, chopped

1 teaspoon finely chopped kaffir lime leaves

2 teaspoons shrimp paste (see note page 77)

serves 4

2 tablespoons peanut or sunflower oil

2 garlic cloves, finely chopped

2 small red or green chillies, deseeded
and finely chopped

12 uncooked king prawns, shelled
and deveined

2 medium onions, halved and
thickly sliced

3 tablespoons Thai fish sauce

2 tablespoons light soy sauce

1 teaspoon sugar

30 fresh holy basil leaves

serves 4

*This is a good dish to try if you are new to the tastes of
Thai food. You will enjoy the combination of fresh prawns
with the strongly aromatic basil. It's easy to vary the
amount of chilli, too, in case very spicy food isn't to your
taste. This is an excellent dish for the beginner cook.*

prawns with chilli and basil

Heat the oil in a wok or frying pan, add the garlic and chillies and fry, stirring
well, until the garlic begins to brown. Stir in the prawns, then add the onions,
fish sauce, soy sauce, sugar and basil, mixing well. Cook until the prawns are
cooked through (it will take just a few minutes – until the prawns are opaque).
Transfer to a dish and serve with other Thai dishes, including rice.

Variations Instead of prawns, use 500 g of pork, beef or chicken, all finely
chopped or minced. In Thailand, the prawns would also be chopped or minced,
but in the West, whole prawns are used instead.

Thai curry is a great flavour hit when you get in from a busy day. This recipe uses a ready-made paste to make everything easier, but your curry will only be as good as your paste. Thai brands are always good, but remember that they are often very hot.

red curry
with prawns and pumpkin

If you remember, put the coconut milk in the refrigerator as soon as you buy it.

When you are ready to start cooking, scrape off the thick coconut cream which usually clings to the lid and put just the cream in a wok or large saucepan over medium heat. Add the curry paste and stir for 1–2 minutes until the paste smells fragrant, then add the sugar and cook for a further 2 minutes until sticky.

Pour in the rest of the coconut milk, add the lemongrass, pumpkin and 100–120 ml water to almost cover the pumpkin. Bring the contents of the wok to a gentle simmer and leave to bubble away gently for 10 minutes, or until the pumpkin is tender.

Add the sugar snap peas and cook for 2 minutes, then add the prawns and cook for a further 2 minutes or until they turn pink. Remove from the heat and stir in the fish sauce. Transfer to bowls and sprinkle with the mint and chilli. Taste and add more fish sauce if necessary. Serve with steamed jasmine rice.

400 ml canned coconut milk

2 tablespoons red curry paste

2 tablespoons palm sugar
or demerara sugar

1 lemongrass stalk, cut in half
and bruised

400 g pumpkin or butternut
squash, peeled, deseeded and
cut into 2-cm chunks

125 g sugar snap peas, cut diagonally

200 g uncooked tiger prawns, shelled,
deveined and butterflied but tails intact

2 tablespoons Thai fish sauce, plus extra
to taste

15 mint leaves, finely shredded

1 large red chilli, deseeded and cut
into thin strips

serves 4

'Tartare' means uncooked and, to serve fish this way, you must use very fresh, sashimi-grade tuna. If you prefer your tuna cooked, sear the whole steak on a preheated stove-top grill pan for 1 minute on each side or until cooked to your liking. However, I do urge you to try it tartare – it is delicious, as the Japanese well know.

chilli tuna tartare pasta

Cook the pasta according to the instructions on the packet.

Meanwhile, heat the oil in a frying pan, add the garlic and fry gently for 2 minutes until lightly golden. Add the chilli, lemon zest and thyme and fry for a further 1 minute.

Drain the pasta, reserving 4 tablespoons of the cooking liquid, and return both to the pan. Stir in the hot garlic oil mixture, the lemon juice, the raw tuna, basil leaves, salt and pepper and a little extra olive oil. Serve at once.

350 g dried fusilli or other pasta

6 tablespoons extra virgin olive oil, plus extra to serve

4 garlic cloves, sliced

1–2 dried red chillies, deseeded and chopped

grated zest and juice of 1 unwaxed lemon

1 tablespoon chopped thyme leaves

500 g tuna steak, chopped

a handful of basil leaves

sea salt and freshly ground black pepper

serves 4–6

Choose lean pork escalopes for this dish and trim off any excess fat. The spicy marinade, which makes the escalopes ideal for barbecuing, can also be brushed onto chicken breasts and other meats. Begin cooking the potatoes before you cook the pork, but don't add the peas and yoghurt until just before serving.

indian grilled pork escalopes
with spiced potatoes and peas

1 tablespoon Madras curry paste

2 tablespoons mango chutney

½ teaspoon ground turmeric

2 tablespoons sunflower oil

4 loin pork escalopes, about 150 g each

150 g cherry tomatoes, on the vine
if available

sea salt and freshly ground
black pepper

spiced potatoes and peas

700 g potatoes, peeled and diced

1 tablespoon sunflower oil

25 g unsalted butter

1 onion, finely chopped

1 garlic clove, crushed

1 teaspoon cumin seeds

150 g frozen petits pois

2 tablespoons Greek yoghurt

sea salt

serves 4

First make the spiced potatoes. Cook the potatoes for 10 minutes in a pan of boiling salted water. Drain in a colander. Heat the oil and butter in a frying pan and add the onion, garlic and cumin seeds. Cook over low heat until the onions have softened. Add the potatoes and 100 ml water, and continue to cook until the potatoes are tender, about 10 minutes.

Meanwhile, preheat the grill to high. Put the curry paste, mango chutney, turmeric and 1 tablespoon oil in a bowl and mix well with salt and pepper. Put the escalopes on a grill rack, season well and brush with half the curry mixture. Arrange the cherry tomatoes on the grill rack alongside the pork and drizzle with the remaining oil.

Cook the escalopes and tomatoes under the preheated grill for 5–6 minutes or until the pork is slightly charred. Brush the other side with the remaining curry mixture and cook for a further 5–6 minutes.

Add the peas and yoghurt to the potatoes just before you are about to serve. Bring to the boil and let bubble for 1 minute.

To serve, put a few generous spoonfuls of the spiced potatoes and peas on warmed serving plates and place a pork escalope on top along with some tomatoes, still attached to their vine if possible.

Since your friends can help themselves and put together their own traditional fajitas, this dish is straightforward to serve. If you prefer a very spicy guacamole, add a couple of extra jalapeño chillies, deseeded and finely chopped.

4 small sirloin steaks, about 2.5 cm thick, each weighing about 200 g

4 tablespoons extra virgin olive oil

1 tablespoon pimentón (Spanish oak-smoked paprika)

1 tablespoon cumin

2 ripe Haas avocados, peeled and stoned

freshly squeezed juice of 1 lime

1 small white onion, finely grated

1 large red onion, cut into petals

1 red or green pepper, deseeded and thinly sliced

3 garlic cloves, cut into slivers

8–12 wheat or corn flour tortillas

sea salt and freshly ground black pepper

to serve

100 g jalapeño chillies, deseeded and chopped

a handful of wild rocket leaves

sour cream or crème fraîche

hot chilli sauce (optional)

a heavy-based stove-top grill pan (optional)

serves 4–6

stir-fried beef fajitas with guacamole and sour cream

Preheat the oven to 170°C (325°F) Gas 3.

Remove any fat from the beef and cut it diagonally, across the grain, to create finger-length strips. Mix together 2 tablespoons oil, the pimentón and cumin in a large bowl. Add the beef pieces and toss until evenly coated in the spiced oil. Set aside while you prepare the guacamole, onions and peppers.

To make the guacamole, roughly mash the avocados in a bowl, leaving some lumps, and stir in the lime juice and white onion. Set aside until needed.

Heat a heavy-based stove-top grill pan or large frying pan over a high heat with the remaining oil and stir-fry the red onion, red or green pepper and garlic for 3–4 minutes, until they start to go limp and the edges begin to char. Remove from the pan and set aside in a warm place.

Wrap the tortillas in foil and place them in the preheated oven to warm, for about 5 minutes. (Alternatively, you can follow the packet instructions for warming them in a microwave.)

Meanwhile, wipe the grill pan clean with kitchen paper. Heat until smoking hot, then drop the strips of meat into the pan over high heat, working in batches and turning them frequently. Each batch should take no more than 1–2 minutes to cook. Season the meat with salt and pepper.

To serve, arrange the beef strips, guacamole, pepper and onion, jalapeño chillies, rocket, sour cream or crème fraîche and hot chilli sauce (if using) in separate bowls. Wrap the tortillas in a cloth napkin (so that they don't dry out and go hard) before bringing them to the table. Let everyone dig in.

4 sirloin or T-bone steaks

olive oil, for brushing

sea salt and freshly ground black pepper

chimichurri parsley base

75 g flat leaf parsley, trimmed of tough stalks and coarsely chopped

2 fat garlic cloves, quartered

½ teaspoon sweet pimentón (Spanish oak-smoked paprika)

¼ teaspoon freshly grated nutmeg

a pinch of ground cinnamon

a pinch of chilli powder or chilli flakes

2 tablespoons freshly squeezed lemon juice

150 ml extra virgin olive oil or corn oil

sea salt, to taste

chimichurri dressing

½ small onion, finely chopped

¾ teaspoon caster sugar

1 teaspoon freshly squeezed lemon juice

1 red pepper, finely chopped (about 6 tablespoons)

¼ teaspoon freshly grated nutmeg

2 tablespoons extra virgin olive oil or corn oil

serves 4

Argentine beef is legendary, thanks to the plentiful grazing land of the pampas and the country's cowboys, the gauchos. Beef is often cooked on a parrilla – a large barbecue grill – and served on its own or with condiments like chimichurri. Serve the steaks with accompaniments such as barbecued vegetables and baked potatoes, which can be cooked in the coals.

argentine barbecued beef
with chimichurri

To make the chimichurri parsley base, put all the ingredients into a blender and work to a smooth sauce. Alternatively, use a mortar and pestle.

Next make the dressing. Put the chopped onion into a bowl, add the sugar and lemon juice and stir well. Cover and set aside for at least 30 minutes. Add the red pepper, nutmeg, oil and 3–4 tablespoons of the chimichurri parsley base. Mix well and set aside. (Save any remaining chimichurri base for use as a pesto-type topping, or pour into ice cube trays, freeze and use for flavouring stocks, soups and stews.)

To prepare the beef, preheat a charcoal grill until very hot (you can add oak or hickory chips if available) and brush the steaks with a little oil. Cook over a fierce heat to begin with, then adjust the rack further away from the fire as soon as the surfaces of the steaks have begun to sear. Cook to your liking, turning once during cooking. Alternatively, cook under a preheated grill or on a stove-top grill pan. Sprinkle with salt and pepper and serve hot with the chimichurri.

Variation Finely chop 1 poblano or other mild green chilli and mix with the chimichurri.

2 tablespoons unsalted butter or ghee (clarified butter)

5 green cardamom pods, bruised

½ cinnamon stick

1.25 kg leg of lamb, well trimmed, boned and cut into chunks, or 800 g boned

5 tablespoons plain yoghurt, whisked

¼ teaspoon cardamom seeds (not pods)

325 ml double cream

sea salt

wet paste

2 fat garlic cloves, sliced

1½ large onions, quartered

4 green chillies, deseeded and coarsely chopped

5 tablespoons ground almonds

to serve

freshly ground white pepper

finely sliced red onion, soaked in a little vinegar

unroasted flaked almonds

serves 4–6

Rich and creamy and steeped in plenty of almond and cardamom sauce, this 'white' dish is a refined affair. The wet paste of garlic, chillies, almonds and onions provides body and a flavour typical of northern India, while the cardamom and cinnamon scent the butter or ghee before other ingredients are added. White pepper is classically used in this dish, in keeping with its colour.

spicy lamb in almond milk

To make the wet paste, put the garlic, onions, chillies and almonds into a blender and blend until smooth, adding a little water to let the blades run. Alternatively, use a mortar and pestle. Set aside.

Melt the butter or ghee in a large heavy-based saucepan and add the cardamom pods and cinnamon stick. Let the spices flavour the butter for 1–2 minutes, then add the wet paste. Sauté the paste for 8 minutes until thickened, stirring frequently to avoid burning.

Add the lamb and stir-fry until brown. Then add the yoghurt and enough water to cover, about 250–325 ml. Whisk well. Heat until almost boiling, stirring constantly. Part-cover with a lid, reduce the heat to low and simmer very gently for 45 minutes. (Lamb cooked over low heat becomes very tender.)

Remove the lid, then stir in the cardamom seeds and salt to taste. Cook for 30 minutes longer. The sauce may look slightly separated, but don't worry.

Finally, stir in the cream, increase the heat and bring to the boil. Reduce the heat and simmer gently for a few minutes to let the sauce thicken slightly. Sprinkle with white pepper, sliced red onion and a few flaked almonds. Serve with boiled rice and naan bread.

1 large sirloin steak, 3–4 cm thick, about 500 g, trimmed of fat

2 tablespoons tamari or other soy sauce

1 teaspoon toasted sesame oil

1–2 teaspoons sugar

1 garlic clove, crushed

3 cm fresh ginger, peeled and grated

2 spring onions, trimmed and chopped

1–2 bird's eye chillies, red or green, deseeded and chopped

a pinch of salt

lettuce leaves, to serve

a stove-top grill pan (optional)

serves 4

This is a Korean delight – as popular with tourists as it is with the locals. Bulgogi is a starter that can be made and served in two ways. The beef strips, always sliced very thinly, can be wide or narrow. The wide ones are served with rice and condiments, while the narrow ones, as here, are rolled up in lettuce leaves – an entirely satisfying way of eating this dish.

bulgogi

Freeze the steak for 1 hour so it will be easy to slice very thinly. Remove the steak from the freezer, then slice very thinly crossways.

To make the marinade, put the tamari or soy, sesame oil and sugar into a bowl and whisk well. Stir in the garlic, ginger, spring onions, chillies and salt, then add the beef strips, mix well to coat, cover and refrigerate for several hours to develop the flavours.

Heat a lightly greased stove-top grill pan or frying pan until very hot. Sear the strips of steak briefly on both sides until just done, working in batches so you don't overcrowd the pan. Either pile onto a serving plate or divide between 4 plates, and serve with lettuce.

100 g raw shelled peanuts

800 g braising beef, well trimmed and cut into thick chunks

1¼ teaspoons tamarind paste

800 ml canned coconut milk

1 large potato, chopped into large chunks

sea salt or fish sauce

mussaman spice paste

2 cardamom pods

½ cinnamon stick

1 teaspoon cumin seeds

1½ tablespoons coriander seeds

½ teaspoon freshly grated nutmeg

5 red bird's eye chillies, deseeded and chopped

1 stalk of lemongrass, very finely chopped

4 garlic cloves, chopped

4 small Thai shallots, coarsely chopped

3 tablespoons chopped coriander stems or roots

a tiny piece of shrimp paste, toasted (see note page 77), or 1 teaspoon anchovy paste

serves 6

This unusual Thai curry is characterized by its thick peanut sauce and it is a firm favourite, inside and outside Thailand. As it is exceedingly rich, serve in smaller portions than you would your average curry.

thai mussaman beef curry

Put the peanuts in a dry frying pan and toast until aromatic. Transfer to a clean tea towel and rub together. The skins should slip off easily. Using a mortar and pestle or food processor, grind the peanuts coarsely and set aside.

Put the beef into a large, heavy-based saucepan, add 500 ml water and bring to the boil. Reduce the heat and simmer for about 1½ hours. Add sea salt or fish sauce to taste.

To make the spice paste, put the cardamom, cinnamon, cumin seeds and coriander seeds in a dry frying pan and toast until aromatic. Using a blender or mortar and pestle, grind to a fine powder. Add the nutmeg, chillies, lemongrass, garlic, shallots, coriander stems and shrimp paste and grind to a thick paste, adding a little water if necessary.

Remove the beef from the saucepan and set aside. The liquid will be substantially reduced, so take care not to let the dish burn at this last stage. You should stir frequently and keep the heat low.

Add the tamarind and half the spice paste and stir. (Freeze the remaining paste for future use.) Stir the coconut milk into the sauce. Return the beef to the saucepan, then add the potatoes – if the mixture is looking too dry, add a little extra water. Simmer gently for 20 minutes, stirring frequently. Add the peanuts, mix well and cook for another 1–2 minutes. Serve with rice.

3 tablespoons peanut or vegetable oil

750 g well trimmed boneless pork sparerib, sliced into chunks*

500 ml beef stock

hinleh paste

4–6 red bird's eye chillies, deseeded and chopped

5 garlic cloves, quartered

½ onion, coarsely chopped

5 cm fresh ginger, peeled and grated

¼ teaspoon ground turmeric

2 cm fresh galangal, peeled and grated

1 stalk of lemongrass, very finely chopped

3 anchovies in oil, drained and finely chopped plus a dash of fish sauce, or ½ teaspoon dried shrimp paste, toasted (see note page 77)

to serve

a handful of Thai basil or coriander

2 red bird's eye chillies, finely sliced lengthways

serves 4

This hinleh (curry) is a Burmese speciality and doesn't include the coconut milk so typical of South-east Asian cooking. It does use three root spices from the same family – turmeric, ginger and galangal. If you can't get fresh galangal, use extra fresh ginger instead.

burmese pork hinleh

To make the hinleh paste, put all the ingredients into a blender and grind to a paste, adding a dash of water to let the blades run. Alternatively, use a mortar and pestle.

Heat the oil in a large saucepan and add the paste. Stir-fry for several minutes. Add the pork and stir-fry to seal. Add the stock, bring to the boil, reduce the heat and simmer gently, stirring occasionally, for 40–45 minutes until cooked through but very tender. Sprinkle with the basil and chilli and serve with rice.

*Note Boneless sparerib meat takes longer to cook than leg meat, but doesn't dry out as easily. It gives best results at a lower temperature. Otherwise, you could use the best cut – fillet – for tender, fast-cooking meat.

This Texan classic is justly world famous. Chilli con Carne is almost always made with chilli powder, but it is also good made with crushed dried chillies or sliced fresh ones. For timid tastebuds, adjust the quantity of chillies or chilli powder to suit.

chilli con carne

500 g dried red kidney beans, washed

½ teaspoon salt

2 tablespoons corn oil or beef dripping

2 onions, sliced

3 garlic cloves, sliced

1 kg braising steak, cut into 1.5 cm cubes

2 tablespoons plain flour

2 tablespoons tomato paste

¼–½ tablespoon chilli powder, dried chilli flakes, or 1–4 whole red serrano chillies, deseeded if preferred, and chopped

1 green pepper, deseeded and chopped

¼ teaspoon ground cumin

1 litre beef stock

sea salt, to taste

to serve

a little chopped coriander

sour cream (optional)

serves 4–6

Put the beans in a bowl, cover with cold water and let soak for at least 3 hours or overnight. (If short of time, put them in a saucepan, cover with cold water, bring to the boil, simmer for 2 minutes, remove from the heat, cover and let soak for 1 hour.) When ready to cook, drain, then rinse in cold water.

Put the beans in a saucepan, cover with cold water, bring to the boil and boil hard for 15 minutes to remove the toxins. Drain, cover with fresh water and return to the boil. Simmer for 1–4 hours or until tender (the time depends on the age of the beans): top up with boiling water as necessary. Add ½ teaspoon salt 15 minutes before the end of cooking. Set aside.

Put the oil or dripping in a large frying pan and heat until melted. Add the onion and garlic and cook gently until softened and lightly browned, about 15 minutes. Transfer to a plate and keep warm.

Add the steak cubes to the pan, in batches if necessary – do not crowd the pan. Fry until browned on all sides. Stir in the flour and mix well. Add the tomato paste, chilli, green pepper, cumin and stock and strain in any cooking liquid from the cooked beans. Bring to the boil, transfer to a casserole or saucepan and simmer on top of the stove or in a preheated oven at 150°C (300°F) Gas 2 for 1¼ hours, or until the meat is tender.

Remove from the heat or oven, season to taste, stir in the beans, return to the stove top or oven and cook for a further 30 minutes.

Sprinkle with chopped coriander and top with a spoonful of sour cream, if using. Serve with warmed tortillas or rice.

The biryani is especially popular in North India and Pakistan. It often includes lamb, although chicken is used here. For celebrations, it may have gold or silver leaf on top.

saffron and pistachio biryani

Put the saffron in a large saucepan with 150 ml water and ½ teaspoon of the salt. Bring to the boil, then set aside to cool.

Melt 75 g of the butter in a second saucepan. Add the rice and fry gently, stirring continuously, until the rice is white and opaque, about 5 minutes. Add 1 litre water, 1 teaspoon salt, 1 cinnamon stick, 3 cloves, 1 bay leaf and half the cardamom. Cover, bring to the boil, reduce the heat and simmer until all the water has been absorbed, about 10–15 minutes. (The rice will be slightly undercooked.)

Measure 600 ml by volume of this part-cooked rice and add to the pan of saffron water. Stir well, cover with a lid, bring to the boil and cook for a couple of minutes or until the rice has absorbed all the water. Add 100 ml water to the remaining white rice, stir, cover, bring to the boil and cook for a couple of minutes or until the rice has absorbed all the water. Measure a further 600 ml of this rice and mix it gently with the saffron rice to give a yellow and white mixture. Spread the remaining white rice into a shallow casserole dish and set aside.

Rinse out the saucepan, add 125 g butter and heat gently. Stir in the remaining cinnamon, cloves, bay, cardamom and the cumin and fry to release the aromas.

Meanwhile, put the onion, ginger, chillies, garlic and 5 tablespoons water in a blender and purée until smooth. Pour this mixture into the pan of hot spices and heat until the water has boiled away and the butter begins to fry the mixture. Add the chicken and seal all over without browning it or the spices. Add the yoghurt, mint, coriander and remaining salt and cover. Raise the heat and simmer for 20 minutes. (Don't worry when the sauce appears to split and become buttery.) Preheat the oven to 190°C (375°F) Gas 5. Remove the chicken and arrange on top of the rice in the casserole, pour the yoghurt sauce over, cover and cook in the preheated oven for 20 minutes while the rice absorbs the liquid.

Remove from the oven and arrange the bi-coloured rice on top, then put it in the oven for a further 5 minutes to heat through. Serve, topped with the fried onion, nuts, raisins and coriander leaves.

a large pinch of saffron threads

2½ teaspoons salt

200 g butter or ghee (clarified butter)

600 ml basmati rice, measured by volume

2 cinnamon sticks

6 cloves

2 bay leaves

6 green cardamom pods, crushed

1 tablespoon ground cumin

½ onion, sliced

3 cm fresh ginger, peeled and sliced

2 red chillies, deseeded and sliced

3 garlic cloves, crushed

4 chicken breasts, skinned and boned

250 ml plain yoghurt, strained, or Greek yoghurt

1 tablespoon chopped mint

1 tablespoon lightly chopped coriander

to serve

½ onion, fried till crisp, then crumbled

50 g green pistachio nuts, shelled, blanched and peeled

30 g almonds, toasted in a dry frying pan, then sliced

50 g raisins or sultanas, soaked in 2 tablespoons boiling water for 30 minutes

a handful of coriander leaves

serves 4

1 kg leg or shoulder of lamb, boned and cubed

750 ml canned coconut milk

a handful of fresh coconut slivers or 1 tablespoon desiccated coconut

a handful of coriander leaves, to serve

masala paste

6 tablespoons peanut oil

3 onions, chopped

5 cm fresh ginger, peeled and grated

3 large garlic cloves, chopped

1 teaspoon ground cinnamon

1 tablespoon ground cumin

1 tablespoon ground coriander

¼ teaspoon ground cardamom

1 teaspoon ground turmeric

2 teaspoons dried chilli flakes

3 tablespoons vinegar

1 teaspoon salt

tempering

2 tablespoons mustard oil or peanut oil

2 red onions, cut into wedges

2 tablespoons mustard seeds

serves 4

This recipe can be made even richer if you have time to allow the flavours of the masala paste and lamb to consolidate overnight. This hearty lamb dish will still be delicious if you can't wait, however.

spiced lamb with coconut

To make the masala paste, heat the oil in a wok, frying pan or metal casserole dish, add the onions, ginger and garlic and stir-fry until lightly browned. Add the cinnamon, cumin, ground coriander, cardamom, turmeric and chilli flakes and cook until the fragrance is released, 3–4 minutes. Stir in the vinegar and salt.

Add the lamb to the pan and fry, turning frequently, for about 10 minutes until lightly browned on all sides. At this point, you may remove it from the heat, let cool, then chill overnight to marinate and develop the flavours (if time is short, this step may be omitted).

Add about 600 ml of the coconut milk. Add water to cover, heat to simmering, then cook until the meat is tender, about 40 minutes. Stir from time to time to prevent the mixture from sticking to the pan. Stir in the rest of the coconut milk and cook for a further 10 minutes.

Meanwhile, put the coconut in a dry wok or frying pan and stir-fry for a few minutes until lightly golden: take care, the pieces can easily burn. Set aside.

To make the tempering, heat the oil in a wok or frying pan, add the onion and mustard seeds and stir-fry until the onion is softened and dark golden brown around the edges. Remove from the heat.

Transfer the lamb to a serving dish, spoon the tempering over the top and the coconut on top of that. Add the coriander and serve with other Indian dishes.

This is a dish of contrasts. It has a mixture of different textures in the soft noodles and crunchy vegetables, plus both hot and sour flavours.

chilli beef noodles

Put the noodles in a heatproof bowl, cover with boiling water and let soak for 3 minutes. Drain and refresh with cold water, then set aside.

Toss the slices of steak together with the onion, garlic and chilli. Heat the sunflower oil in a non-stick frying pan or wok over high heat. Add the beef mixture and stir-fry for 2 minutes. Mix in the beansprouts and mangetout and cook, stirring, for 1 minute.

Stir the noodles into the pan with the lime juice and fish sauce and heat through. Pile into 2 serving bowls and serve immediately, topped with the chopped coriander.

100 g rice noodles

150 g rump steak, trimmed and thinly sliced

1 red onion, thinly sliced

2 garlic cloves, thinly sliced

1 red chilli, deseeded and thinly sliced

1 teaspoon sunflower oil

100 g beansprouts, rinsed

75 g mangetout, halved diagonally

1 tablespoon freshly squeezed lime juice

1 tablespoon Thai fish sauce

2 tablespoons chopped coriander, to serve

serves 2

An easy dish to prepare and cook, this is a suitable recipe for those new to Thai cooking. The combination of garlic and chilli ensures a very hot and traditional Thai flavour.

2 tablespoons peanut or sunflower oil

3 large garlic cloves, finely chopped

500 g lean pork, thinly sliced

2 tablespoons Thai fish sauce

2 tablespoons light soy sauce

2 large red chillies, thinly sliced

sliced spring onions, to serve

serves 4

pork with garlic
and fresh chilli

Heat the oil in a wok or frying pan until a light haze appears. Add the garlic and stir-fry until golden brown. Add the pork and and stir-fry briefly.

Add the fish sauce, soy sauce and chillies, stirring briskly all the time. By now the pork should be cooked through. Spoon onto a serving dish and top with sliced spring onions. Serve with other Thai dishes, including rice, noodles and perhaps fresh pickle.

Variations Instead of the pork, use a similar quantity of thinly sliced chicken or beef, or shelled and deveined prawns.

8 large or 12 medium lamb cutlets, trimmed of fat

2 tablespoons extra virgin olive oil, plus extra to drizzle

1 teaspoon cumin seeds

800 g canned chickpeas, drained and rinsed

300 g cherry tomatoes, on the vine

4 tablespoons chopped coriander

sea salt and freshly ground black pepper

marinade

2 tablespoons extra virgin olive oil

2 tablespoons chopped mint

finely grated zest of 1 unwaxed lemon

5 tablespoons freshly squeezed lemon juice

1 teaspoon chilli powder

1 garlic clove, peeled and crushed

serves 4

The lemony, minty marinade is perfect here with lamb cutlets that are grilled to rosy perfection. The marinade is also very good with chicken, prawns and fish. Mashing the chickpeas by hand produces a less gluey result than using a food processor.

cumin-spiced lamb cutlets
with chickpea mash and roasted vine tomatoes

To make the marinade, combine the olive oil, mint, lemon zest and 1 tablespoon of the juice, the chilli powder and garlic in a large bowl. Add the lamb cutlets, season well and toss. If you have time, marinate for an hour; if not, continue.

Heat ½ tablespoon of the olive oil in a frying pan over medium heat, add the cumin seeds and stir for 30 seconds until fragrant. Tip in the chickpeas and toss in the oil for 1 minute. Stir in the remaining lemon juice and 100 ml water, cover and simmer for 10 minutes until softened. Preheat the grill to high.

Put the lamb cutlets on a baking sheet lined with aluminium foil and grill for 5–6 minutes until charred around the edges. Turn over, add the tomatoes (halving any large ones), drizzle with the remaining olive oil, season and grill for a further 5–6 minutes.

Mash the chickpeas with a potato masher until you get a chunky purée. Add the coriander, season to taste and stir. Transfer to bowls and top with 2 or 3 lamb cutlets. Drizzle with olive oil and lamb juices.

3 lemongrass stalks

200 g minced lamb

2 shallots, finely chopped

2 teaspoons chopped parsley

2 teaspoons chopped coriander

½ teaspoon ground allspice

1 small red chilli, deseeded and finely chopped

flour, for dusting

2 tablespoons sunflower oil

½ small red pepper, deseeded and cut into thin strips

12 white mini pitas, warmed

12 crisp baby lettuce leaves

12 small sprigs coriander

minted crème fraîche

125 ml half-fat crème fraîche

2 tablespoons mint, chopped

salt and freshly ground black pepper

serves 4 (makes 12)

These fragrant mini-kebabs are popular in Morocco and Tunisia. The lemongrass skewers add a fragrance and opulence to the koftas, but you can use pre-soaked wooden cocktail sticks if preferred.

lamb kofta wraps
with minted crème fraîche

Slice the lemongrass in half widthways, then lengthways to make 12 sticks. In a bowl, mix the minced lamb, shallots, parsley, coriander, allspice and chilli together. Divide into twelve and with lightly floured hands shape into 5 cm long finger shapes. Thread the koftas onto the lemongrass skewers.

In a small bowl mix the crème fraîche and mint together and season.

Heat the oil in a frying pan and fry the koftas for 4–5 minutes, turning to brown on all sides. At the same time add the pepper strips and cook for 3–4 minutes, to soften and brown slightly.

Open each pita bread lengthways, place a lettuce leaf in each and add a kofta, a few strips of red pepper and a sprig of coriander. Serve the wraps with the minted crème fraîche.

Tagines made with meatballs (kefta) do not require long cooking. Generally, the sauce is prepared first and the meatballs are poached in it, until just cooked. This popular meatball recipe is light and lemony and is delicious served with a salad and couscous tossed with chilli and herbs.

tagine of spicy kefta
with lemon

To make the kefta, pound the minced meat with your knuckles in a bowl. Using your hands, lift up the lump of minced meat and slap it back down into the bowl. Add the onion, parsley, cinnamon, cumin, coriander and cayenne, and season to taste with salt and black pepper. Using your hands, mix the ingredients together and knead well, pounding the mixture for a few minutes. Take pieces of the mixture and shape them into little walnut-sized balls, so that you end up with about 16 kefta. (These can be made ahead of time and kept in the refrigerator for 2–3 days.)

Heat the oil and butter together in a tagine or heavy-based casserole. Stir in the onion, garlic, ginger and chilli and sauté until they begin to brown. Add the turmeric and half the coriander and mint, and pour in roughly 300 ml water. Bring the water to the boil, reduce the heat and simmer, covered, for 10 minutes. Carefully place the kefta in the liquid, cover and poach the kefta for about 15 minutes, rolling them in the liquid from time to time so they are cooked well all over. Pour over the lemon juice, season the liquid with salt and tuck the lemon segments around the kefta. Poach for a further 10 minutes.

Sprinkle with the remaining coriander and mint and serve hot.

1 tablespoon olive oil

1 tablespoon butter or ghee (clarified butter)

1 onion, roughly chopped

2–3 garlic cloves, halved and crushed

a thumb-sized piece of fresh ginger, peeled and finely chopped

1 red chilli, thinly sliced

2 teaspoons ground turmeric

a small bunch of coriander, roughly chopped

a small bunch of mint, chopped

freshly squeezed juice of 1 lemon

1 unwaxed lemon, cut into 4 or 6 segments, with pips removed

kefta

450 g finely minced beef or lamb

1 onion, finely chopped or grated

a small bunch of flat leaf parsley, finely chopped

1–2 teaspoons ground cinnamon

1 teaspoon ground cumin

1 teaspoon ground coriander

½ teaspoon cayenne pepper, or 1 teaspoon paprika

sea salt and freshly ground black pepper

a tagine (optional)

serves 4–6

1 lemongrass stalk

500 g minced pork

125 g minced pork belly

25 g breadcrumbs

6 kaffir lime leaves, very thinly sliced

2 garlic cloves, crushed

2 cm fresh ginger, peeled and grated

1 red chilli, deseeded and chopped

2 tablespoons Thai fish sauce

oil, for brushing

to serve

lettuce leaves

a handful of herb leaves, such as mint, coriander and Thai basil

sweet chilli sauce

4 wooden skewers soaked in cold water for 30 minutes

serves 4

Like many Vietnamese dishes, these delicious pork balls are served wrapped in a lettuce leaf with plenty of fresh herbs and sweet chilli sauce.

vietnamese pork balls

Using a sharp knife, trim the lemongrass stalk to about 15 cm, then remove and discard the tough outer leaves. Chop the inner stalk very finely.

Put the minced pork and pork belly and breadcrumbs into a bowl, then add the lemongrass, lime leaves, garlic, ginger, chilli and fish sauce and mix well. Let marinate in the refrigerator for at least 1 hour.

Using your hands, shape the mixture into 20 small balls and carefully thread 5 onto each of the soaked wooden skewers. Preheat the grill to hot, or prepare the barbecue, then brush the grill rack with oil. Cook the skewers under the grill or over hot coals for 5–6 minutes, turning halfway through until cooked.

Serve the pork balls wrapped in lettuce leaves with the herbs and chilli sauce.

This is the easiest and most delicious noodle dish in the world! Don't worry about deep-frying the noodles – they quickly puff up in a most satisfying fashion.

thai mee krob

Mix the dressing ingredients together in a small saucepan and cook, stirring, just until dissolved. Keep hot. Line 4 serving bowls with crumpled kitchen paper.

Heat the vegetable oil in a wok, add the curry paste and cook for 1–2 minutes until the aromatics have been released. Add the pork strips and stir-fry until crispy, then add the prawns and stir-fry for about 1 minute until they turn opaque. Transfer to a dish and keep warm.

Wipe out the wok, fill one-third full of peanut oil and heat to 190°C (375°F) or until a small piece of noodle will fluff up immediately.

Add a handful of noodles. Let puff and cook for 1 minute, then carefully turn over with tongs and cook the other side for 1 minute. Remove to one of the paper-lined bowls. Reheat the oil and repeat with the remaining noodles, reheating and skimming the oil as necessary. When all are ready, turn the noodles over in the bowls and discard the kitchen paper. Divide the pork, prawns and toppings between the bowls, drizzle the dressing over and serve with chopsticks.

*Note Mild orange mussaman curry paste is sold in larger supermarkets and Thai shops. If unavailable, use another Thai curry paste, such as red or green.

1 tablespoon vegetable oil

1 tablespoon mussaman curry paste*

4 pork chops, deboned and sliced

4–8 uncooked prawns, shelled and deveined, tail fins intact, halved lengthways

peanut oil, for frying

4 bundles wide dried ricestick noodles or fine rice vermicelli noodles

dressing

125 ml white rice vinegar

125 g palm sugar or brown sugar

4 tablespoons soy sauce

4 tablespoons Thai fish sauce

toppings

8 spring onions, sliced diagonally

6 baby Thai shallots, sliced (optional)

1 small packet beansprouts, trimmed

2 red chillies, deseeded and sliced crossways

sprigs of coriander

serves 4

chicken dishes

8 boneless chicken thighs or 4 breasts, skin on

3 teaspoons turmeric

3 whole star anise, crushed

3 garlic cloves, crushed

5 cm fresh ginger, thinly sliced

grated zest of 1 lime and 1 tablespoon freshly squeezed lime juice

2 tablespoons Thai fish sauce

1 tablespoon dark soy sauce

2 tablespoons chilli oil

1 tablespoon peanut oil

5 snake beans, cut in 5 cm lengths (optional)

500 ml canned coconut milk

sliced red chillies, to serve

serves 4

This quick and easy Thai stir-fry makes a perfect midweek supper dish to share with friends.

thai marinated chicken
stir-fried in chilli oil

Place the chicken, skin side down, in a shallow non-metallic container. To marinate, rub in the turmeric, star anise, garlic, ginger and lime zest, then sprinkle with the lime juice, fish sauce, soy sauce and half the chilli oil. Turn the chicken pieces in the mixture to coat well, cover and leave in the refrigerator to marinate for 1 hour or overnight, turning at least once.

When ready to cook, drain, slice into 1 cm strips and reserve the marinade.

Heat a wok, add the peanut oil and remaining chilli oil and heat until hot, then add the chicken pieces, skin side down. Cook at a high heat for 1–2 minutes until the skin is crispy, then turn down the heat and continue cooking until browned. Turn the pieces over and brown the other side.

Add the snake beans, reserved marinade and the coconut milk and stir well. Bring to the boil, stirring slowly, lower the heat, then simmer for 10–15 minutes until the chicken is tender. Sprinkle with sliced red chilli and serve with jasmine rice.

Chicken satay is one of the most popular Thai dishes. You can use it as part of a barbecue menu, whether Oriental or not, or as a party snack – the sticks make this very easy to nibble with drinks, and the peanut sauce is good as a dip with other foods, such as crudités.

chicken satay

To make the peanut sauce, heat the oil in a frying pan until a light haze appears. Add the chopped garlic and fry until golden brown. Add the curry paste, mix well and cook for a few seconds. Add the coconut milk, mix well and cook for a few seconds more. Add the stock, sugar, salt and lemon juice. Cook for 1–2 minutes, constantly stirring. Add the ground peanuts, stir thoroughly and pour the sauce into a bowl. Set aside until ready to serve.

To make the satays, toast the coriander and cumin seeds gently in a small frying pan without oil for about 5 minutes, stirring and shaking to make sure they don't burn. Remove from the heat and grind with a mortar and pestle to make a fine powder. (Use ready-ground spices if you are short of time.)

Using a sharp knife, cut the chicken breasts lengthways into thin strips, about 5 mm wide. Put them in a bowl and add the ground toasted seeds, fish sauce, salt, peanut oil, curry powder, turmeric, coconut milk and sugar. Mix thoroughly and refrigerate for at least 8 hours or overnight (you can prepare them in the morning to serve in the evening).

Preheat a grill, charcoal grill or barbecue. Thread 2 pieces of the marinated chicken onto each skewer – not straight through the meat, but rather as if you were gathering a piece of fabric in a zigzag fashion. Grill the satays until the meat is cooked through – about 6–8 minutes – turning to make sure they are browned on both sides. Serve with the peanut sauce and lemon or lime wedges.

2 teaspoons coriander seeds

2 teaspoons cumin seeds

4 skinless chicken breasts

2 tablespoons Thai fish sauce

1 teaspoon salt

4 tablespoons peanut or sunflower oil

1 tablespoon curry powder

1 tablespoon ground turmeric

125 ml coconut milk

3 tablespoons sugar

lemon or lime wedges, to serve

peanut sauce

2 tablespoons peanut or sunflower oil

3 garlic cloves, finely chopped

1 tablespoon panaeng curry paste or Thai red curry paste

125 ml coconut milk

250 ml chicken stock

1 tablespoon sugar

1 teaspoon salt

2 tablespoons freshly squeezed lemon or lime juice

4 tablespoons crushed roasted peanuts

18–20 wooden skewers, soaked in cold water for about 30 minutes

serves 4

4 chicken quarters (breasts or legs)

2 tablespoons sunflower oil

1 teaspoon Chinese five-spice powder

3 cm fresh ginger, peeled and grated

$^1/_2$ teaspoon salt

3 tablespoons honey

1$^1/_2$ tablespoons dark soy sauce

ginger bok choy

3 tablespoons dark soy sauce

1 tablespoon sweet chilli sauce

2 tablespoons sunflower oil

2 teaspoons toasted sesame oil

3 cm fresh ginger, peeled and thinly
sliced into matchstick strips

8 small bok choy, halved, well washed
and patted dry with kitchen paper

serves 4

Chinese five-spice powder is used widely in Asian cooking. It is made up of cassia bark (similar to cinnamon), cloves, fennel, star anise and Szechuan pepper.

roast five-spice chicken
with ginger bok choy

Preheat the oven to 300°C (400°F) Gas 6.

Wash and dry the chicken pieces and put in a roasting tin. Put the oil, five-spice powder, ginger and salt in a bowl, mix well, then brush all over the chicken. Roast in the preheated oven for 25 minutes.

Put the honey and soy sauce in a small saucepan and heat until the honey has melted. Stir well, then brush all over the chicken to form a glaze. Return to the oven and roast for a further 10 minutes until the skin is crisp and golden.

To prepare the bok choy, put the soy sauce, chilli sauce and 4 tablespoons water into a bowl and mix well.

Heat the two oils in a wok or large frying pan, add the ginger and stir-fry for 30 seconds. Add the bok choy and continue to stir-fry for a further 2 minutes. Add the soy sauce mixture, cover and simmer gently for 2 minutes, then serve with the chicken.

The authentic flavour of this curry comes from using fresh spices and the heady, slightly sour taste of bay leaves. Chicken thigh fillets work better here than breast meat as they are harder to overcook.

chicken and lentil curry
with cucumber yoghurt

Melt the butter in a deep frying pan, add the onions and fry, stirring, over medium heat. Once they are sizzling, cover with a lid, reduce the heat and cook for 10–15 minutes, stirring occasionally.

When the onions have softened, add the garlic and garam masala, cook for a further 3–4 minutes until the spices start to release their aroma and the onions are beginning to turn golden. If you are using chicken thighs, add them now and cook for 5–6 minutes. Add the passata, bay leaves, lentils and stock. If you are using chicken breast, add it now. Cover with a lid and simmer for 15 minutes until the lentils are tender.

To make the cucumber yoghurt, put the yoghurt in a small dish, add a good pinch of salt and stir in the cucumber.

When the curry is cooked, season generously with salt and freshly ground black pepper (lentils tend to absorb a lot of seasoning so don't be stingy). Transfer to bowls, scatter with coriander, if using, and serve with a dollop of the cucumber yoghurt. Serve with mango chutney and warm chapattis.

25 g butter or ghee (clarified butter)

2 large onions, thinly sliced

2 garlic cloves, peeled and crushed

1 1/2 tablespoons garam masala (or 1/4 teaspoon ground nutmeg, 1/2 teaspoon each ground cinnamon and ground pepper, 1 teaspoon ground cumin and 10 cardamom pods, crushed)

500 g chicken thigh fillets or breast fillets, cut into chunks

300 g tomato passata

8 bay leaves

100 g red lentils

400 ml chicken stock

sea salt and freshly ground black pepper

coriander leaves, to serve (optional)

cucumber yoghurt

140 ml pot plain yoghurt

1/4 cucumber, cut into ribbons or chopped

serves 4

2 tablespoons rice wine, such as
Chinese Shaohsing or Japanese mirin

2 teaspoons cornflour

350 g skinless chicken breasts

175 g Chinese dried egg noodles

3 tablespoons peanut or sunflower oil

3 cm fresh ginger, peeled and thinly
sliced into shreds

125 g mangetout, finely sliced

4 tablespoons chopped garlic chives
or chives

125 g cashew nuts, toasted in
a dry frying pan, then chopped

sauce

100 ml chicken stock

2 tablespoons dark soy sauce

1 tablespoon freshly squeezed
lemon juice

1 tablespoon sesame oil

2 teaspoons soft brown sugar

serves 4

*Most noodle dishes take just a matter of minutes to cook,
which makes them ideal for quick midweek suppers and
a welcome alternative to pasta.*

gingered chicken noodles

Put the rice wine and cornflour into a bowl and mix well. Cut the chicken into
small chunks, add to the bowl, stir well and set aside to marinate while you
prepare the remaining ingredients.

Soak the noodles according to the instructions on the packet, then drain and
shake dry.

Put all the sauce ingredients into a small bowl and use a fork or small whisk to
mix well.

Heat half the oil in a wok or large frying pan, then add the marinated chicken
and stir-fry for 2 minutes until golden. Remove to a plate and wipe the pan
clean. Add the remaining oil, then the ginger and mangetout and fry for
1 minute. Return the chicken to the pan, then add the noodles and sauce.
Heat through for 2 minutes.

Add the garlic chives and cashew nuts, toss and serve.

This is a dish from south-east India, where the people have a penchant for fiery food. It includes plenty of chillies combined with coriander seeds.

chettinad chicken

Using a mortar and pestle, blender or spice mill, grind the dried chillies and toasted coriander seeds to a fine powder. Set aside.

To make the tarka spice-fry, put the oil or ghee in a frying pan and heat well. Add the turmeric, peppercorns, fennel and cumin seeds. Let sizzle briefly, then add the onion. Sauté for a few minutes, then add the ginger. Sauté for a further 6 minutes or so, until the onion is soft. If necessary, add a dash of water to prevent the mixture sticking to the pan.

Add the chicken and toss well to coat with the tarka. Sauté until the chicken begins to brown. Add enough water to cover, about 325 ml, then the tomatoes. Bring to the boil, reduce the heat and gently simmer until the chicken is cooked, about 8–10 minutes. A few minutes before the end of cooking time, stir in 1¼ tablespoons of the reserved ground chilli-coriander spice blend (or more, to taste) and season with salt. Put the tamarind paste into a bowl, add a ladle of liquid, stir to dissolve, then stir into the pan. Sprinkle with the coriander and top with the chillies, if using, then serve with the yoghurt.

8 large dried red chillies

2 tablespoons coriander seeds, toasted in a dry frying pan

4 skinless chicken breasts, cut into chunks

3 tomatoes, chopped

2 teaspoons tamarind paste

sea salt

tarka spice-fry

2 tablespoons peanut oil or ghee (clarified butter)

¼ teaspoon turmeric

4 black peppercorns

¼ teaspoon fennel seeds

¼ teaspoon cumin seeds

1 onion, finely chopped

3 cm fresh ginger, peeled and grated

to serve

a handful of coriander leaves, chopped (optional)

2–4 green chillies, halved and deseeded (optional)

plain yoghurt

serves 4

This recipe is based on the classic Asian salt 'n' pepper squid. It makes a delicious chicken dish, guaranteed to become a family favourite at barbecues. Serve with a squeeze of fresh lime and chilli sauce.

pepper 'n' spice chicken

To make the fragrant Asian rub, put the whole spices in a dry frying pan and toast over medium heat for 1–2 minutes or until golden and aromatic. Remove from the heat and let cool. Transfer to a spice grinder and crush to a coarse powder. Alternatively, use a mortar and pestle. Put the spices into a bowl, add the garlic, lime zest and salt and mix well. Set aside to infuse until ready to use.

Cut the chicken into 12 portions and put into a dish. Add the rub and sesame oil and work well into the chicken pieces. Let marinate in the refrigerator for 2 hours, but return to room temperature for 1 hour before cooking.

Preheat the barbecue, then cook the chicken over medium hot coals for 15–20 minutes, turning after 10 minutes, until the chicken is cooked through and the juices run clear when the thickest part of the meat is pierced with a skewer. Squeeze with lime juice, let cool slightly and serve with sweet chilli sauce.

1 small chicken

2 tablespoons toasted sesame oil

1–2 limes, cut into wedges

sweet chilli sauce, to serve

fragrant asian rub

4 whole star anise

2 teaspoons Szechuan peppercorns

1 teaspoon fennel seeds

2 small pieces of cassia bark or 1 cinnamon stick, broken

6 cloves

2 garlic cloves, finely chopped

grated zest of 2 limes

1 teaspoon salt

an outdoor barbecue

serves 4

4 chicken legs (thigh and drumstick)

lemon or lime wedges, to serve

jerk seasoning paste

3–4 habanero chillies, deseeded

1 teaspoon chopped thyme

3 garlic cloves, coarsely chopped

1 bay leaf

1 teaspoon allspice berries (about 20)

$\frac{1}{4}$ teaspoon freshly grated nutmeg

3 spring onions, chopped

2 plum tomatoes, skinned (fresh or canned)

freshly squeezed juice of $\frac{1}{2}$ lime

80 ml peanut oil

$\frac{1}{2}$ teaspoon salt

serves 4

There are as many jerk chicken recipes in Jamaica as there are cooks, but all include the fiery Scotch bonnet chilli or the closely related habanero, plus a good dose of native allspice. Traditionally grilled over wood, this recipe can easily be cooked in the oven or on the barbecue.

jerk chicken

To make the jerk seasoning paste put all the ingredients in a mortar and pestle and grind to a smooth paste.

Cut slashes in the chicken legs and spread with half the jerk seasoning paste. Rub the paste all over and into the slashes, cover and marinate in the refrigerator for at least 2 hours or overnight.

Preheat the oven to 200°C (400°F) Gas 6. Put the chicken legs skin side down into a roasting tin. Roast them in the preheated oven for 40–45 minutes or until crisp and cooked through, turning halfway through the cooking time and coating with the remaining marinade.

To cook on a barbecue, preheat a charcoal grill until very hot. Cook the chicken over high heat to begin with, then adjust the rack further away from the fire as soon as the surfaces of the chicken have begun to brown. Cook for 15–20 minutes or until done, turning frequently and basting with the remaining marinade. You must cook poultry thoroughly so there is no pink inside: if you have an instant-read thermometer, it should read 75°C (165°F) when inserted into the thickest part of the thigh.

Serve hot with lemon or lime wedges on the side for squeezing.

Chapattis are unleavened breads typically served as an accompaniment to spicy dishes in northern India, so they make the perfect wraps for this spicy Indian chicken topped with yoghurt and cucumber relish.

indian chicken wraps
with minted cucumber relish

Preheat the oven to 200°C (400°F) Gas 6.

Cut the chicken fillets into strips. In a shallow dish, mix the curry paste, yoghurt and oil together. Add the chicken and toss to coat. Cover and leave to marinate for 30 minutes, or up to 4 hours, if time allows.

To make the relish, put the yoghurt in a bowl with the cucumber, spring onions, mint and cumin. Mix together and season with black pepper. Chill.

Transfer the chicken pieces to a non-stick baking tray and bake for 15 minutes, or until the chicken juices run clear. Meanwhile, wrap the chapattis in foil and place in the oven to warm for the last 5 minutes, while the chicken is cooking.

Cut the chapattis in half. Top each half with a few strips of chicken and some spinach leaves, roll up and secure with a cocktail stick. Serve 2 per person, along with a spoonful of the minted cucumber relish.

250 g skinless chicken breast fillets

2 tablespoons tandoori or tikka masala curry paste

3 tablespoons natural yoghurt

2 teaspoons sunflower oil

4 chapattis

20 g baby spinach leaves

minted cucumber relish

150 g natural yoghurt

$1/4$ cucumber, deseeded and diced

3 spring onions, chopped

2 tablespoons mint, chopped

$1/2$ teaspoon ground cumin

freshly ground black pepper

cocktail sticks

serves 4

3 tablespoons sunflower oil

450 g skinless chicken breast fillets, cut into strips

1 large onion, chopped

1 red chilli, deseeded and finely chopped

1 garlic clove, crushed

2 tablespoons tomato purée

400 g can chopped tomatoes

410 g can pinto beans, drained and rinsed

1 tablespoon chopped coriander

8 corn tortillas, warmed

150 ml soured cream

75 g mature Cheddar cheese, grated

salt and freshly ground black pepper

shredded spring onions, to serve

serves 4–6

Corn tortillas, pinto beans and chillies are synonymous with Mexican cooking. This recipe combines chicken with a fiery tomato sauce as a filling for the soft tortillas, which are topped with soured cream and Cheddar cheese before baking. It makes a perfect lunch or supper dish served with a crisp leaf salad.

chilli chicken enchiladas

Preheat the oven to 190°C (375°F) Gas 5.

Heat 2 tablespoons of the oil in a large non-stick frying pan, add the chicken and stir-fry for 4–5 minutes, or until golden. Remove with a slotted spoon, put into a large bowl and set aside.

Add the remaining oil to the pan, then the onion and fry for 5 minutes. Add the chilli and garlic and fry for 1–2 minutes more, or until the onions are soft and golden. Stir in the tomato purée, canned tomatoes and 100 ml cold water. Cook for 2–3 minutes and season with salt and freshly ground black pepper.

Add just under half the sauce to the chicken with the beans and coriander and mix together. Spoon 2 heaped tablespoons of the chicken mixture onto the middle of each warmed tortilla and roll up to enclose the filling. Place seam-side down in a greased baking dish and top with the remaining tomato sauce.

Spoon the soured cream along the centre of the tortillas and sprinkle with the grated cheese. Bake in the preheated oven for 15–20 minutes or until golden and bubbling. Sprinkle over the spring onions and serve.

This Moroccan stew is both fruity and spicy, and the rosemary and ginger give it a delightful aroma. Serve it with couscous and a leafy green salad.

spicy chicken tagine
with apricots, rosemary and ginger

Heat the oil and butter in a tagine or heavy-based casserole. Stir in the onion, chopped rosemary, ginger and chillies and sauté until the onion begins to soften. Stir in the halved rosemary sprigs and the cinnamon sticks. Add the chicken thighs and brown them on both sides. Toss in the apricots with the honey, then stir in the plum tomatoes with their juice. (Add a little water if necessary, to ensure there is enough liquid to cover the base of the tagine and submerge the apricots.) Bring the liquid to the boil, then reduce the heat. Cover with a lid and cook gently for 35–40 minutes.

Season to taste with salt and pepper. Shred the larger basil leaves and leave the small ones intact. Sprinkle them over the chicken and serve the dish immediately.

2 tablespoons olive oil with a knob of butter

1 onion, finely chopped

3 sprigs of rosemary, 1 finely chopped, the other 2 cut in half

40 g fresh ginger, peeled and finely chopped

2 red chillies, deseeded and finely chopped

1–2 cinnamon sticks

8 chicken thighs

175 g ready-to-eat dried apricots

2 tablespoons clear honey

400 g canned plum tomatoes with juice

sea salt and freshly ground black pepper

a small bunch of green or purple basil leaves

a tagine (optional)

serves 4

3 tablespoons vegetable oil

1 onion, roughly chopped

2 garlic cloves, crushed

1 tablespoon Madras curry paste

1 tablespoon tomato purée

400 g canned chopped tomatoes
(flavoured with mixed herbs,
if available)

1 teaspoon red wine vinegar

125 g chargrilled red peppers, chopped

125 g courgettes, diced

450 g cooked chicken, cut into
bite-sized pieces

sea salt and freshly ground black pepper

coriander sprigs, to garnish

serves 6

You can make this tantalizingly spicy chicken jalfrezi in less time than you might wait for a takeaway delivery. Use a jar of prepared chargrilled peppers and look out for good-quality curry pastes in supermarkets. Go for a hot variety containing spices such as chilli, cumin, coriander, tamarind and turmeric. Serve with jasmine rice and ready-cooked poppadoms.

chicken jalfrezi

Heat the oil in a large frying pan, reduce the heat and add the onion and garlic. Sauté over medium heat until golden. Add the curry paste and cook for 1 minute to cook off the spices.

Add the tomato purée, chopped tomatoes, vinegar and 200 ml water to the frying pan. Bring to the boil and simmer, uncovered, for 5 minutes.

Add the chargrilled red peppers and diced courgettes and cook for a further 5 minutes until the courgettes are tender. Stir in the chicken pieces and season with salt and pepper. Simmer gently for another 6–7 minutes, or until the chicken is piping hot.

Just before serving, garnish with coriander sprigs. Serve with jasmine rice and poppadoms.

You can add your choice of vegetables to this basic curry recipe, such as sliced mushrooms, trimmed French beans, fresh spinach, bamboo shoots or sticks of courgette and carrot – it's perfect for using up odds and ends. Jasmine or fragrant rice is a delicately scented white rice native to Thailand. If you are very short on time, use one of the excellent brands that is microwavable in the packet.

quick thai chicken curry

To make the jasmine rice, put the rice in a large pan that has a tight-fitting lid. Add 375 ml cold water, the butter and salt. Bring it to the boil, and turn down the heat to a simmer. Cook over low heat, covered, for 20 minutes or until the rice has absorbed all the liquid (add a little more water if the rice is not yet tender).

Meanwhile, pour the coconut milk into a saucepan and gently bring it to near boiling. Remove the saucepan from the heat and stir in the Thai curry paste. Put to one side. Pour the oil into a large frying pan or wok and stir-fry the chicken pieces over high heat until golden, about 2 minutes.

Pour the warm, spiced coconut milk over the fried chicken pieces and add the kaffir lime leaf purée and fish sauce. Add any vegetables you are using at this stage. Stir and simmer gently for about 12 minutes, or until everything is cooked through.

Remove the cooked rice from the heat and let sit for 5 minutes. Fluff it up with a fork just before serving. Scatter the basil over the curry and serve it with a small bowl of rice on the side.

400 ml canned coconut milk

50 g Thai green curry paste

1 tablespoon sunflower oil

1 chicken breast (about 400 g), cut into bite-sized pieces

$1/2$ teaspoon kaffir lime leaf purée

1 teaspoon Thai fish sauce

100 g mixed vegetables of your choice (see introduction)

a handful of basil leaves

jasmine rice

200 g Thai jasmine or fragrant rice

25 g unsalted butter

a pinch of sea salt

serves 2

4 skinless, boneless chicken breasts, about 130 g each

grated zest and freshly squeezed juice of 1 unwaxed lemon

1 tablespoon olive oil

1 teaspoon ground cumin

1 teaspoon paprika or smoked paprika

2 garlic cloves, crushed

2 tablespoons chopped parsley

2 tablespoons chopped coriander

sea salt and freshly ground black pepper

tomato pilaff

1 large aubergine, cut into 1 cm dice

4 ripe tomatoes, chopped

1 teaspoon cumin seeds

2 garlic cloves, crushed

2 teaspoons tomato purée

150 g basmati rice

410 g canned chickpeas, drained and rinsed

250 ml boiling water

1 teaspoon olive oil

serves 4

Chermoula is a fragrant North African paste that is often used as a marinade for fish, but works just as well with chicken. Instead of tomato pilaff, you could serve this with plain rice if you are short of time.

chermoula chicken
with tomato pilaff

Toss the diced aubergine for the pilaff with a pinch of salt and set aside in a colander for 15 minutes to draw out the excess liquid.

Lightly slash the chicken breasts so that the marinade will be able to permeate the meat. Mix the lemon zest and juice with the olive oil, cumin, paprika, garlic, parsley, coriander and seasoning. Rub into the chicken, cover and set aside in a baking dish in a cool place.

To make the pilaff, put the tomatoes, cumin seeds, garlic, tomato purée and 2 tablespoons water in a large saucepan and simmer rapidly for 5–6 minutes until thick and quite dry. Stir in the rice, chickpeas, boiling water and a pinch of salt. Bring back to the boil, stir the rice once, then cover the pan tightly and leave to simmer on the lowest heat for 20 minutes.

Preheat the oven to 200°C (400°F) Gas 6. Squeeze the liquid from the aubergines and pat dry on kitchen paper. Toss with the olive oil and spread out on a baking sheet. Put on the highest shelf in the preheated oven, with the dish of chicken on the shelf below. Cook both for 15–18 minutes, stirring the aubergine halfway through cooking to brown evenly.

Stir the roasted aubergine into the tomato pilaff, then serve with the chermoula chicken breasts on top. Serve with runner beans or another green vegetable.

vegetarian dishes

1 tablespoon olive oil

1 onion, finely chopped

1 garlic clove, crushed

1 tablespoon harissa paste

400 g canned chickpeas, drained
and rinsed

400 g canned chopped tomatoes
(flavoured with garlic or mixed herbs,
if available)

125 g halloumi cheese, cut into cubes

100 g baby spinach leaves

freshly squeezed juice of ½ lemon

sea salt and freshly ground
black pepper

freshly grated Parmesan cheese, to serve

serves 2

Halloumi is a firm Cypriot cheese that is delicious eaten when hot and melting. It has a reasonably long shelf-life before it is opened, which means you can keep a pack tucked away in the fridge. Harissa is a fiery chilli paste used in North African cooking – add more than the tablespoon here if you like your food very spicy.

harissa-spiced chickpeas
with halloumi and spinach

Pour the oil into a large pan and gently sauté the onion and garlic until softened. Add the harissa paste, chickpeas and chopped tomatoes. Bring to the boil and let simmer for about 5 minutes.

Add the halloumi cheese and spinach, cover and cook over a low heat for a further 5 minutes. Season to taste and stir in the lemon juice. Spoon onto serving plates and sprinkle with the Parmesan cheese. Serve immediately with a crisp green side salad.

This tasty dish makes a delicious TV dinner or can be served as a midweek supper for friends and family.

vegetable burritos

Preheat the oven to 200°C (400°F) Gas 6.

To make the salsa, mix all the ingredients together. Cover and chill until ready to use.

Put the tomatoes in a saucepan with the garlic, chilli powder, oregano and tomato purée. Bring to the boil, reduce the heat and simmer for 10 minutes, until the mixture reduces slightly and begins to thicken.

Meanwhile, heat the oil in a separate saucepan. Add the peppers and sauté for about 5 minutes, until soft. Add the peppers to the tomato mixture. Put the refried beans in a saucepan and heat gently, stirring frequently until piping hot.

Wrap the tortillas in foil and warm in the preheated oven for 6–7 minutes, until soft and piping hot, or heat according to the instructions on the packet. Remove from the oven and put the tortillas on 4 serving plates. Spread each tortilla with a thick layer of beans, then 1 tablespoon of the tomato and pepper mixture, a quarter of the cheese, 1 tablespoon of the salsa and 1/2 tablespoon of crème fraîche. Sprinkle with coriander, fold and serve immediately.

400 g canned chopped tomatoes

3 garlic cloves, crushed

1 tablespoon mild chilli powder, or to taste

a pinch of dried oregano

1 tablespoon tomato purée

1 tablespoon olive oil

1 yellow pepper, deseeded and sliced

1 green pepper, deseeded and sliced

400 g canned refried beans, or canned borlotti or pinto beans, drained, rinsed and mashed

4 large wheat flour tortillas

100 g extra-mature Cheddar cheese, coarsely grated

2 tablespoons half-fat crème fraîche

2 tablespoons chopped coriander

sea salt and freshly ground black pepper

salsa

1/2 large red onion, chopped

2 tomatoes, chopped

1/2 green chilli, deseeded and finely chopped

1 tablespoon freshly squeezed lime juice

1 tablespoon chopped mint

serves 4

If you are looking for a tasty and filling meal, try this recipe. Sweet potatoes make a nutritious alternative to ordinary potatoes and as they stay moist during cooking, there is no need to add extra butter.

baked sweet potatoes
with mexican beans

Preheat the oven to 200°C (400°F) Gas 6.

Scrub the potatoes and prick them all over with a fork. Cook the potatoes in the preheated oven for 1–1¼ hours, or until soft. Alternatively, wrap the potatoes in kitchen paper and microwave each one on high for 3½–4 minutes, or until soft. Let the potatoes stand for 1 minute.

Heat the oil in a non-stick saucepan. Add the onion, garlic and chillies, red wine vinegar and Worcestershire sauce. Sauté until the onions are soft, about 5 minutes. Add the tomatoes to the pan, bring to the boil, lower the heat and simmer for 10 minutes. Add the beans, stir and cook for a few minutes more until they are piping hot. Stir in the coriander.

Cut the sweet potatoes in half. Put 2 halves on each serving plate and spoon the Mexican beans over the top. Sprinkle with some grated Cheddar cheese, if using, and serve immediately.

4 sweet potatoes, about 200 g each

1 tablespoon olive oil

1 onion, finely chopped

2 garlic cloves, crushed (optional)

2 red chillies, deseeded and finely chopped

2 tablespoons red wine vinegar

1 tablespoon Worcestershire sauce

600 g canned chopped tomatoes

400 g canned mixed beans, drained and rinsed

1 tablespoon chopped coriander

50 g extra-mature Cheddar cheese, grated, to serve (optional)

serves 4

50 g polenta grain

50 g plain flour

3 eggs

200 ml semi-skimmed milk

2 garlic cloves

2 red onions

12 patty pan squash

2 red peppers

1 pickled red jalapeño chilli

1 tablespoon olive oil, plus extra
for frying

1 bunch of coriander

salt

tomato salsa

4 ripe tomatoes

2 spring onions

1 red chilli

2 tablespoons red wine vinegar

serves 4

These pretty yellow pancakes, made with polenta, have a sweet, nutty texture. Add a dollop of soured cream and this dish could be served by itself for lunch, or as a starter.

corn crêpes
with chilli vegetables and tomato salsa

To make the crêpes, put the polenta grain, plain flour and a pinch of salt in a bowl, then beat in the eggs and milk to form a smooth batter. Set aside.

To make the filling, crush the garlic, slice the onions and cut the squash in quarters. Deseed and chop the red peppers and pickled chilli. Heat 1 tablespoon olive oil in a pan, add the garlic, onions, squash, peppers, chilli and a pinch of salt, and fry gently until tender.

To make the salsa, roughly chop the tomatoes and finely chop the spring onions. Deseed and roughly chop the red chilli, then mix all the ingredients together and chill until ready to use.

To cook the crêpes, heat the oil in an 18 cm frying pan. Add a ladle of batter and swirl the pan around so the mixture covers the base. Cook until the surface bubbles and the base is browned, then turn and brown the other side. Remove and set aside in a warm place while you cook the remaining crêpes.

Roughly chop the coriander. Spoon the filling into the crêpes, top with coriander and serve with the tomato salsa.

The potato, known as aloo in several Indian languages, is an important ingredient for the large vegetarian Hindu population. It has revolutionized nutrition in high mountain areas, where the potato yield is more reliable than the grain crops it replaced.

2 large aubergines

750 g waxy potatoes, peeled and cut into 1 cm cubes

6–8 tablespoons vegetable oil

1 tablespoon cumin seeds

1 teaspoon black mustard seeds

1 teaspoon sesame seeds

1 onion, finely chopped

1–2 garlic cloves, crushed

1 teaspoon grated fresh ginger

1 green chilli, deseeded and finely chopped

$\frac{1}{2}$ teaspoon ground turmeric

1 teaspoon ground coriander

$\frac{1}{2}$ teaspoon salt, plus extra for sprinkling

1–2 tablespoons lemon or lime juice

to serve

4 tablespoons plain yoghurt

garam masala, for sprinkling

2 tablespoons chopped fresh coriander

serves 4

indian dry potato curry in aubergine shells

Cut the aubergines in half lengthways and, using a spoon, scoop out the flesh leaving a 5 mm shell. Cube the flesh into 1.5 cm dice. Sprinkle the inside of the aubergine shells with salt and place in a colander, cut side down. Spread the aubergine cubes on a plate or tray or in a colander and sprinkle with more salt. Leave for about 30 minutes, then rinse well and pat dry with kitchen paper.

Preheat the oven to 190°C (375°F) Gas Mark 5. Bring a pan of lightly salted water to the boil, add the potato cubes and cook for 5 minutes. Drain well and let cool. Place the aubergine shells, cut side up, on a baking sheet, brush with 2 tablespoons of the oil and cook in the preheated oven for about 10–15 minutes, until softened. Remove from the oven and turn the aubergine shells upside down on a plate to drain off any excess oil.

Heat another 2 tablespoons of the oil in a large frying pan, add the cumin, mustard and sesame seeds and when they start to pop add the onion, garlic, ginger and chilli. Stir-fry for about 2–3 minutes then add the aubergine cubes. Cook, stirring occasionally, for 4–5 minutes or until they are just cooked, adding more oil as needed.

Stir in the turmeric, ground coriander and salt, then add the potatoes and stir-fry for 5–6 minutes until the potatoes are golden. Remove from the heat and stir in the lemon or lime juice. Taste and adjust the seasoning.

Put the aubergines back on the baking sheet, cut side up. Divide the potato mixture evenly between them and return to the oven for 10 minutes to heat through. Serve with the yoghurt and sprinkle with a little garam masala and the chopped fresh coriander.

125 g yellow lentils

3 tablespoons oil

1/2 teaspoon mustard seeds

1/2 teaspoon fenugreek seeds

1 teaspoon grated fresh ginger

1 teaspoon crushed garlic

1 teaspoon chilli powder

1 1/2 teaspoons ground coriander

1/2 teaspoon ground turmeric

4 tomatoes, skinned and chopped

1 teaspoon salt

750 g floury potatoes, peeled and diced

to serve

3 tablespoons chopped coriander, plus extra sprigs, to garnish

1/2 teaspoon garam masala

serves 4

Rice and lentils is a staple meal for millions of Indians and Nepalis. In this recipe, potatoes are added to that traditional duo. They are particularly desirable for their ability to absorb the wonderful flavours of Indian spices.

indian potato curry
with yellow lentils

Wash the lentils well in several changes of water.

Heat the oil in a large saucepan, over a low heat. Add the mustard and fenugreek seeds. When they begin to pop, stir in the ginger and garlic and fry for 30 seconds.

Add the chilli powder, ground coriander and turmeric and stir-fry for a further 30 seconds. Add the tomatoes and lentils to the pan, cover with 600 ml water, add the salt, bring to the boil, reduce the heat, cover and simmer for 20–30 minutes or until the lentils are just soft. Add the potatoes and simmer over a low heat for 10–15 minutes or until tender. Taste and adjust the seasoning.

Sprinkle with chopped coriander and garam masala, add sprigs of fresh coriander and serve with basmati rice, naan bread or both.

We have Mexico to thank for the introduction of chillies to the rest of the world. This recipe calls for smoky chipotle chilli, as well as cumin seeds.

burritos with black beans
and avocado salsa

Put 2 of the garlic cloves and the beans into a saucepan, add enough water to cover the beans by 3 cm, bring to the boil, reduce the heat, cover and cook for 1½–2 hours or until the beans are very tender (cooking time depends on the age of the beans). Drain the beans, reserving the cooking liquid.

Crush the remaining garlic and chop the chillies. Heat the oil in a large saucepan and add the chillies and cumin. Fry for 20 seconds, then add the onion. Fry for about 5 minutes, then add the crushed garlic. Cook for a further 3–4 minutes or until the onion is soft. Add the drained beans, together with a little of their cooking liquid to keep them moist. Continue to cook, stirring frequently. Season with salt and pepper and mash well, adding enough liquid to make a chunky paste. Cover.

To make the salsa, scoop out the avocado flesh and cut into smallish chunks. Put it into a bowl with the lime juice, tossing well so the avocado doesn't discolour. Add the red onion and cherry tomatoes, then stir in the sugar and coriander. Mix well, cover and set aside.

Wrap the tortillas in foil and warm in a preheated oven for 6–7 minutes, until soft and piping hot, or heat according to the instructions on the packet. Gently reheat the beans, add the spring onions and coriander and stir gently. Put a small portion of the beans onto each tortilla and carefully roll into a sausage shape. Put a little salsa onto each plate. Let guests help themselves to the shredded lettuce and crème fraîche or Greek yoghurt.

3 garlic cloves

200 g dried black beans, soaked overnight and drained

2 chipotle chillies

2 tablespoons corn or olive oil

1½ teaspoons cumin seeds

1 onion, finely chopped

6 large corn or wheat flour tortillas

2–4 spring onions, chopped

a handful of coriander, chopped

sea salt and freshly ground black pepper

avocado salsa

1 avocado

freshly squeezed juice of 1 lime

1 large red onion, chopped

10 cherry tomatoes, quartered

½ teaspoon sugar

4 tablespoons chopped coriander

to serve

a handful of shredded lettuce

crème fraîche or Greek yoghurt

serves 6 as a starter or 3 as a main course

Szechuan peppercorns are an important spice in Chinese cookery, included in the well-known blend of Chinese five-spice. They are available in Chinese stores. Not related to black pepper, Szechuan peppercorns are unusual in appearance and taste. They are used in a simple stir-fry here, where their effect can be appreciated. Serve this dish with noodles or rice.

vegetable stir-fry
with szechuan peppercorns

Discard any shiny black inner seeds from the peppercorns. Toast the peppercorns in a small frying pan over low heat for 1–2 minutes until aromatic. Using a mortar and pestle, grind to a coarse powder.

Heat the peanut oil in a wok and add the spring onions and garlic. Stir-fry over medium-high heat for 1 minute. Add the pepper, carrot, baby corn, lemon juice and 1 tablespoon of the soy sauce and stir-fry for 2–3 minutes.

Add the broccoli, sugar snap peas, ground Szechuan pepper and the remaining soy sauce. Stir-fry briefly, cover and cook for 4–5 minutes or until the vegetables are tender but still firm. Uncover and add the sesame oil. Stir and serve hot with a small dish of ground Szechuan pepper for guests to help themselves.

1 teaspoon Szechuan peppercorns, plus extra to serve

2 tablespoons peanut oil

4 spring onions, chopped

2 garlic cloves, sliced

1 small red pepper, deseeded and thinly sliced lengthways

1 carrot, thinly sliced lengthways into matchsticks

18 baby sweetcorn, chopped into 3

freshly squeezed juice of $1/2$ lemon

3–4 tablespoons dark soy sauce

1 small head of broccoli, broken into florets

14 sugar snap peas, trimmed

1 tablespoon toasted sesame oil

serves 4

This Provençal-style tian is cooked in a wide, shallow, open casserole dish. The chorizo adds an extra dimension for non-vegetarians but is optional.

capsicum chilli tian
with goats' cheese

4 red peppers

2 yellow or orange peppers

125 ml extra virgin olive oil, plus extra for brushing and drizzling

2 small mild chorizo sausages, finely sliced (optional)

a handful of basil leaves, plus extra for scattering

12 cherry tomatoes, halved

2 red onions, finely chopped

1–2 medium-hot red chillies, deseeded and finely sliced

about 250 g mature goats' cheese, cut into 12 chunks

lemon wedges, to serve

sea salt flakes and freshly ground black pepper

pesto

a large bunch of basil

a large handful of parsley leaves

75 ml olive oil

4 tablespoons pine nuts, about 25 g

2 garlic cloves, crushed

75 g grated Parmesan cheese

serves 4

To make the pesto, put the basil, parsley, olive oil, pine nuts and garlic in a blender and process until smooth. Add the Parmesan, then blend again. Set aside until needed. Preheat the oven to 200°C (400°F) Gas 6.

Cut the peppers in half lengthways through the stalk. Carefully remove the cores. Put the peppers in a plastic bag, add the 125 ml olive oil and salt and pepper, then shake until well coated with oil.

Brush a shallow casserole dish with extra olive oil and add the peppers, cut side up, cramming them close together. Put a slice of chorizo (if using), a basil leaf, a halved cherry tomato, a spoonful of pesto, some onion, a little chilli and a chunk of goats' cheese in each pepper half. Drizzle more olive oil over the top.

Cook in the preheated oven for 30 minutes, or until all the peppers are tender and crispy brown at the edges and the cheese is melted and bubbling.

Serve on small plates with extra basil leaves scattered over the top, wedges of lemon for squeezing and a salad. Char-grilled Italian bread is perfect for mopping up the delicious juices.

Curry originated in the Indian subcontinent and migrated eastwards towards Thailand long before it travelled west to Europe and North America. Thai curries are generally even hotter and more flavourful than their Indian cousins. Choose a brand of red curry paste that is made in Thailand if you can.

vegetable curry

Put the oil in a saucepan, heat well, then quickly stir in the curry paste. Add the coconut cream, mixing well. Add the vegetable stock and stir briefly.

Add the longbeans, carrots, corn, cauliflower, lime leaves, chillies, soy sauce, sugar, salt and aubergines. Stir well, then cook for a few minutes until the vegetables are tender.

Add the basil leaves, stir once, then ladle into a bowl and serve with jasmine rice.

2 tablespoons peanut or sunflower oil

2 tablespoons Thai red curry paste

600 ml coconut cream

600 ml vegetable stock

4 Chinese longbeans, cut into 2.5 cm pieces

4 carrots, cut into matchsticks

5 baby sweetcorn, cut into 2.5 cm pieces

80 g cauliflower, cut into florets

4 kaffir lime leaves, coarsely chopped

2 large red or green chillies, coarsely sliced

3 tablespoons light soy sauce

2 teaspoons sugar

$^{1}/_{2}$ teaspoon salt

6 small round green aubergines, quartered

30 basil leaves

serves 4

sunflower oil, for greasing

large wheat flour tortillas

Cheddar cheese, grated, feta cheese, crumbled, or cream cheese

fillings

chopped tomatoes

chopped spring onions

chopped red chillies

sliced pickled jalapeño chillies

sliced pickled onions

finely sliced courgettes

sliced mushrooms

chopped peppers

chopped avocado

pitted black olives

mashed, canned refried beans, black beans, pinto beans or borlotti beans

ground cumin

pimentón (Spanish oak-smoked paprika)

to serve (optional)

chopped coriander

sour cream, crème fraîche or plain yoghurt

serve 1 quesadilla per person

Quantities for these excellent snacks are not given here as there's no need, just pile on as much filling as you like. Fried, grilled or baked, this Mexican snack also makes excellent party food.

quesadillas

Lightly grease a large frying pan with 1 teaspoon of oil. Lay a tortilla flat in the pan and cover with cheese and 4 or 5 fillings of your choice. Top with a second tortilla and press down gently. Cook over a moderate heat until the bottom tortilla is golden and crisp, about 5–7 minutes. Cover with a plate, turn the pan over and lift it off. Slide the inverted quesadilla back into the pan and cook as before. Cut into triangles to serve.

Serve the quesadillas warm with chopped coriander and sour cream, if using.

Variation To grill or bake, put a tortilla on a lightly greased baking sheet, top with cheese, preferably Cheddar, and add 4 or 5 fillings of your choice. Cook under a hot grill or in a preheated oven at 180°C (350°F) Gas 4 for 10 minutes or until the cheese is golden.

Based on a charred, then puréed aubergine, this unusual curry is incredibly good. It can be made in advance and, in fact, improves by being left overnight so that all the spicy flavours can develop.

charred aubergine and coconut curry

To make the spice paste, dry-toast the spice seeds in a frying pan, shaking until they pop and turn lightly golden. Transfer to a blender or spice grinder, add the remaining ingredients and 6 tablespoons water to loosen the mixture and grind to a smooth paste. Set aside.

Roast the aubergine directly over a high gas flame until charred and softened, about 15 minutes. Alternatively, roast in a preheated oven at 220°C (425°F) Gas 7 for about 40 minutes. Let cool, then peel and discard the skin. Don't worry if a few charred bits remain – this will add extra flavour.

Heat the oil in a large, heavy-based saucepan, add the onion and cook until softened. Add the spice paste and stir for 2 minutes to release the aromas, then add the pepper, sweet potatoes, courgettes and chickpeas. Cover and cook, stirring occasionally, for 10 minutes. Add the tomatoes and 250 ml water, then bring to the boil and simmer, uncovered, for about 20 minutes.

Put the peeled aubergine in a blender, add the coconut milk and pulse to a coarse purée. Add to the pan and bring back to a simmer. Add salt, if necessary. Cook for 10 minutes, then remove from the heat, cover and let stand for at least 30 minutes or preferably overnight.

Reheat, then top with coriander sprigs and serve with steamed basmati rice, yoghurt and mango chutney.

1 medium aubergine, about 250 g

2 tablespoons vegetable oil or ghee (clarified butter)

1 red onion, chopped

1 red pepper, chopped

250 g sweet potatoes or yams, peeled and cut into cubes

1 medium courgette, about 200 g

400 g canned chickpeas, drained and rinsed

400 g canned chopped tomatoes

250 ml canned coconut milk

sprigs of coriander, to serve

sea salt, to taste

spice paste

1 tablespoon cumin seeds

1 tablespoon coriander seeds

seeds from 10 cardomom pods

$^1/_2$ teaspoon fenugreek seeds

5 cm fresh ginger, peeled and grated

4 garlic cloves

1 teaspoon turmeric

1 teaspoon dried chilli flakes

1 tomato, cut into quarters

2 teaspoons sea salt

1 teaspoon sugar

serves 4–6

500 g halloumi cheese, sliced

2 red onions, halved and cut into wedges

1 red pepper, deseeded and sliced

1 yellow pepper, deseeded and sliced

1 green pepper, deseeded and sliced

1 medium or 2 small courgettes, quartered lengthways and cut into chunks

200 g button mushrooms

8–10 large wheat flour tortillas

marinade

2 garlic cloves

1 tablespoon coarse sea salt

grated zest of 2 limes

freshly squeezed juice of 4 limes

a handful of coriander, chopped

$\frac{1}{2}$ teaspoon dried oregano

$\frac{1}{2}$ teaspoon dried chilli flakes

1 teaspoon cumin seeds

1 teaspoon sugar

1 tablespoon white wine vinegar

125 ml dark rum

125 ml olive oil

to serve

ready-made guacamole

tomato salsa (page 201)

sour cream, crème fraîche or thick plain yoghurt

serves 4–6

Fajitas – usually made with beef or chicken – are utterly delicious and can be adapted easily for vegetarians, using halloumi. This firm cheese from Cyprus is unique; it won't melt when fried and develops a delicious crisp crust. Eat the fajitas as soon as you make them; the halloumi loses tenderness if left for too long after cooking.

halloumi fajitas

To make the marinade, crush the garlic and salt to a paste in a mortar and pestle. Transfer to a bowl, add the remaining ingredients, except the oil, and whisk together. Add the oil in a steady stream, whisking until the mixture has emulsified. Put the halloumi in a shallow dish, add enough marinade to cover and turn until coated. Put the onions, peppers, courgettes and mushrooms in a bowl, add the remaining marinade and mix well. Cover both dishes and let marinate in the refrigerator for at least 30 minutes.

Preheat the oven to 150°C (300°F) Gas 2. Stack the tortillas, wrap in foil and put in the preheated oven for about 15 minutes until warm. Meanwhile, heat a large frying pan or wok until very hot, add the marinated vegetables and liquid and stir-fry until the juices have evaporated and the vegetables are golden and slightly caramelized, about 20 minutes. Transfer to a heatproof dish, cover and keep it warm in the oven. Drain the halloumi, discarding the marinade. Put the slices in the pan or wok in a single layer. Cook over a moderate heat for about 10 minutes, turning halfway through cooking, until golden.

Serve the tortillas, vegetables and cheese separately, so that people can make their own fajitas. To assemble, put a warm tortilla on a plate, add a spoonful of vegetables to one half and top with halloumi. Bring the uncovered half of the tortilla up over the filling, then tuck the corners underneath the fajitas. Serve with guacamole, salsa and lots of sour cream, crème fraîche or yoghurt.

150 g jasmine or long-grain rice, washed

150 ml vegetable stock

150 ml groundnut oil

4 large eggs

2 garlic cloves, peeled and crushed

4 spring onions, sliced

1 teaspoon sesame oil

1 tablespoon light soy sauce

a good pinch of white pepper

2 tablespoons oyster sauce

2 red chillies, deseeded and finely chopped

a handful of coriander leaves

serves 2

A dish from a restaurant in Sydney was the inspiration for this recipe. To eat, tear up the egg with chopsticks and mix the frazzled whites and molten yolks into the rice.

deep-fried eggs
with rice, chilli and oyster sauce

Put the rice and stock in a small saucepan, cover and cook over high heat on a small ring. Once it is boiling, reduce the heat as low as it will go and leave to bubble away gently for 8–10 minutes, or until the rice has swelled and absorbed all the water. Turn off the heat and leave it to steam for another 10 minutes.

Pour the groundnut oil into a wok or large saucepan and heat until hot – throw in a cube of bread and if it browns in 10 seconds, the oil is hot enough. Crack 2 of the eggs into a dish, then gently slide them into the wok. It will hiss and splutter so stand back for a couple of seconds. Cook for 1–2 minutes until the whites are set but the yolks still oozy, then transfer with a slotted spoon onto a plate. Cook the remaining eggs in the same way.

Pour away all but 1 tablespoon of the groundnut oil (you can bottle it and use it again once cool) and add the garlic. Cook until it is starting to colour, then tip in the cooked rice and half the spring onions. Stir-fry briskly, then add the sesame oil, soy sauce and white pepper. Give it a good stir, then transfer to 2 bowls. Put 2 eggs on each mound of rice, drizzle with oyster sauce and sprinkle over the chillies, the remaining spring onions and the coriander leaves.

Pulses such as split peas and lentils are a good source of protein for vegetarians and they work well as a base for hot chillies. In India, dhal is a traditional accompaniment to rice, flatbreads and curried vegetables or meat.

spinach dhal
with toasted coconut

375 g yellow split peas, washed

½ teaspoon ground turmeric

1 teaspoon salt

3 tablespoons vegetable oil

1 teaspoon cumin seeds

1 cinnamon stick

3–5 dried, hot red chillies

250 g fresh spinach leaves

2 tablespoons shredded coconut, or coconut flakes, toasted (optional)

serves 4

Put the split peas in a pan, add the turmeric and about 1.2 litres water. Bring to the boil, then cover with the lid slightly ajar. Reduce the heat and simmer for about 20 minutes, then add salt and cook for about 15–20 minutes more, until the split peas are cooked and tender, and have absorbed all the liquid.

Heat the oil in a small frying pan until very hot, add the spices and gently fry to release the aromas, then add the spinach and gently sauté for a few minutes until the leaves turn bright green.

Heap the spiced spinach on heated plates and spoon the yellow dhal beside. Sprinkle with shredded or toasted coconut, if using, and serve.

This country-style Moroccan dish is typical of regions where meat is regarded as a luxury by most families. Pulses of all kinds and, in particular, chickpeas, provide the nourishing content of these dishes. Serve with plain yoghurt and warmed flatbread.

carrot and chickpea tagine
with turmeric and coriander

Heat the oil in a tagine or heavy-based casserole, add the onion and garlic and sauté until soft. Add the turmeric, cumin, cinnamon, cayenne, black pepper, honey and carrots. Pour in enough water to cover the base of the tagine and cover with a lid. Cook gently for 10–15 minutes.

Toss in the chickpeas, check that there is still enough liquid at the base of the tagine, cover with the lid, and cook gently for a further 5–10 minutes. Season with salt, sprinkle the rosewater and coriander leaves over the top and serve with lemon wedges.

3–4 tablespoons olive oil

1 onion, finely chopped

3–4 garlic cloves, finely chopped

2 teaspoons ground turmeric

1–2 teaspoons cumin seeds

1 teaspoon ground cinnamon

$^1/_2$ teaspoon cayenne pepper

$^1/_2$ teaspoon ground black pepper

1 tablespoon dark, runny honey

3–4 medium carrots, sliced on the diagonal

800 g canned chickpeas, drained and rinsed

1–2 tablespoons rosewater

a bunch of coriander leaves, finely chopped

lemon wedges, to serve

sea salt

a tagine (optional)

serves 4

index

credits

photographs

KEY: ph= photographer, a=above,
b=below, r=right, l=left, c=centre.

Peter Cassidy
Pages 1, 2, 3, 5, 6, 8, 9bl both,
10, 13, 21, 23, 33, 35, 36, 39, 46,
47a&tc all, 49, 50, 53, 54, 57, 61,
67, 69, 70, 75, 80, 81l, 81br, 81c,
83, 99, 101, 102, 105, 117, 118,
123, 124, 125l,125b, 125r, 125cr,
127, 128, 131, 132, 135, 136,139,
149, 162, 163l, 163cl, 167, 168,
172, 175, 178, 186, 189, 192,
193 all, 195, 205, 211, 213, 217,
229, 231

William Lingwood
Pages 9ar all, 24, 27, 29, 43,
44–45, 106, 109, 110, 125a, 140,
143, 144, 152, 155, 181, 182, 214

William Reavell
Pages 81b, 81ar, 112, 115, 121, 147,
150, 163cr, 163a, 171, 191, 225

Nicki Dowey
Pages 62, 64, 84, 87, 89, 90,
196, 199

James Merrell
Endpapers, pages 40, 93, 94, 97,
200, 203, 226

Jeremy Hopley
Pages 30, 47b, 76, 79, 161, 165

Philip Webb
Pages 58, 72, 218, 221, 222, 232

Martin Brigdale
Pages 157, 163b, 185, 235

Peter Myers
Pages 17, 18, 206, 208

Ian Wallace
Pages 14, 158, 177

recipes

Ghillie Basan
Carrot and chickpea tagine
with turmeric and coriander
Spicy chicken tagine with
apricots, rosemary and ginger
Tagine of spicy kefta with lemon

Celia Brooks Brown
Charred aubergine and
coconut curry
Chilli greens with garlic crisps
Halloumi fajitas
Mexican gazpacho
Quesadillas
Thai coleslaw

Tamsin Burnett-Hall
Chermoula chicken with
tomato pilaff
Chilli beef noodles
Goan prawn curry
Spiced salmon with chickpea dhal

Manisha Gambhir Harkins
African seafood kebabs with
piri piri basting oil
Andalusian chickpea soup with
chorizo, paprika and saffron
Argentine barbecued beef
with chimichurri
Bulgogi
Burmese pork hinleh
Burritos with black beans and
avocado salsa
Cajun-spiced chowder with
corn and bacon
Chettinad chicken
Chilito
Coconut prawn masala
Indonesian beef and coconut soup
Jerk chicken
Moroccan grilled fish with
chermoula spice paste
Salsa roja
Singapore turmeric laksa
South Indian spiced rice
Spicy lamb in almond milk
Stir-fried peanut prawns with
coriander noodles
Thai mussaman beef curry
Vegetable stir-fry with Szechuan
peppercorns
Vegetarian cashew salad with
tamarind dressing
Vietnamese spiced squid

Tonia George
Chicken and lentil curry with
cucumber yoghurt
Cumin-spiced lamb cutlets
with chickpea mash and roasted
vine tomatoes

Deep-fried eggs with rice,
chilli and oyster sauce
Red curry with prawns
and pumpkin

Clare Gordon Smith
Caribbean curry
Corn crêpes with chilli vegetables
and tomato salsa
Prawn brochettes with chilli,
papaya and mango salsa
Spinach dhal with toasted
coconut
Steamed mussels in a red
chilli broth
Thai seafood curry with coriander
and coconut milk
Vegetable fritters with coriander
chilli mint raita

Rachael Anne Hill
Asian salmon with rice noodles
Baked sweet potatoes with
Mexican beans
Chicken and chilli chickpea salad
Chilli scallops with spaghetti
Prawn and butter bean rice
Prawn and mango salad
Spicy tuna steaks with
pepper noodles
Vegetable burritos

Caroline Marson
Chicken jalfrezi
Chilli scallops with leeks and
lime crème fraîche
Chilli tiger prawn salad
Harissa-spiced chickpeas with
halloumi and spinach
Indian grilled pork escalopes with
spiced potatoes and peas
Quick Thai chicken curry
Stir-fried beef fajitas with
guacamole and sour cream
Tom yum prawn noodle soup

Annie Nichols
Indian dry potato curry in
aubergine shells
Indian potato curry with
yellow lentils
Mini potato roti with coconut
and mint chutney
Tortitas de papa with chorizo
and corn salsa verde

Elsa Petersen-Scheplern
Indonesian beef satays
Indonesian gado-gado
Singapore coconut laksa
Singapore pork satays
Tamarind fish laksa
Thai marinated chicken stir-fried
in chilli oil

Thai mee krob
Thai pork balls with chilli
dipping sauce
Thai spicy prawn salad
Vietnamese chicken salad with
chilli-lime dressing

Louise Pickford
Chilli tuna tartare pasta
Curried red lentils
Gingered chicken noodles
Oysters with spicy chorizo
Pepper 'n' spice chicken
Prawns with chilli oil and
pistachio and mint pesto
Quick vegetarian mole
Roast five-spice chicken with
ginger bok choy
Thai prawn cakes with chilli jam
Vietnamese pork balls

Rena Salaman
Feta and chilli dip
Spicy hoummus

Jennie Shapter
Chilli chicken enchiladas
Indian chicken wraps with minted
cucumber relish
Lamb and couscous wraps with
harissa dressing
Lamb kofta wraps with minted
crème fraîche
Mini spring rolls with chilli
dipping sauce

Fiona Smith
Crispy chilli beef wontons
Egg rolls with chilli tofu
Spicy crumbed squid strips

Sonia Stevenson
Capsicum chilli tian with goats'
cheese
Chilli con carne
Fish mollee
Thai green fish curry
Kerala coconut chilli prawns
Saffron and pistachio biryani
Spiced lamb with coconut

Vatcharin Bhumichitr
Chicken satay
Chicken wings with lemongrass
and sweet and hot sauce
Green curry with prawns
Pork with garlic and fresh chilli
Prawns with chilli and basil
Vegetable curry
Vegetables with spicy Thai dip of
young chillies